THE AFELD FAMILY:

OUR JOURNEY FROM GERMANY TO AMERICA

THE AFELD FAMILY:

OUR JOURNEY FROM GERMANY TO AMERICA

DAVID A. HOFFMAN

KNIGHTSBRIDGE
Genealogy Services

2015

First Printing: 2014

Second edition: 2015

ISBN 978-0-9862134-0-3 (paperback/black & white)

Other editions:
ISBN 580-0-1114069-4-5 (hardcover/color)
Available at www.lulu.com

Knightsbridge Genealogy Services
P.O. Box 320431
Tampa, Florida 33679

www.mygenealogyconsultant.com
info@mygenealogyconsultant.com

CONTENTS

Dedication vi

Acknowledgements vii

Forward viii

Introduction ix

My Story 1

The Afeld Family of Fulda, Germany 31

The Afeld Brothers Come to America:

      Josef F. Afeld 37

      Franz Wilhelm Afeld 45

The First Generation in America:

      Eugene Franz Louis Afeld.. 57

      Norman Afeld 69

      Charles Oscar Richard Afeld 91

      Amelia Afeld 97

      Norma Julia Afeld 107

Allied Families:

      The Sandbichler Family of Bavaria, Germany 111

      The Ancestry of Anna Maria Drinnenberg of Hünfeld, Germany 119

      The Ancestry of Olga C. Antony of Christiania, Norway 131

ACKNOWLEDGEMENTS

D.J. Holt, for assistance in translating the old church records from Latin.

Stefan Auth, for research in the German Diocesan archives.

Members of the Afeld, Afield, and Marshall families who shared their memories, stories, and family photos.

The staff of the New York City Municipal Archives for finding those unfindable records.

DEDICATION

To our immigrating ancestors, Franz Afeld, Theresa Sandbichler, Carl Antony and Helga Olsen, who had the courage and strength of character to make the journey and lay the foundation for our family in America.

FORWARD

The research and writing of this book was commissioned by Walter Edward Afield, M.D. in March of 2013. The research took about 18 months and compiling and writing the book took an additional six months.

The book is organized to follow the Afeld/Afield family line. Following an autobiography written by Walter Afield in chapter one, the remaining chapters are grouped into four sections:

- The Afeld family in Fulda, Germany – those who did not immigrate.

- The Afeld brothers come to America, with chapters for Josef and Franz, the two brothers who did immigrate.

- The first generation of the descendants of Franz Afeld – his children - with a chapter for each and their descendants.

- Allied families – those who married into the Afeld family, with chapters for the Sandbichler, Drinnenberg, and Antony families.

While every effort was made to include as much of the research as possible and for it to be as up to date as possible, a family history is never "finished". It changes every day, as older records are discovered and as present day descendants go about their lives. It is the hope of Dr. Afield and the author that subsequent generations of the family will continue to research the family and add to its rich heritage.

David A. Hoffman
November 2014

INTRODUCTION

For the longest time, I thought my ancestors were Jewish. Probably because my father hated Jews and early in his life changed his name from Afeld to Afield, adding an "I" because "Afeld sounded too Jewish." In reality, I knew nothing about the family on his side and decided I would research that. I learned a lot more when I began to spend time with Hollis, my half-brother, in the 1970's. I had come back to Tampa to take a position as Professor and Chairman of the Department of Psychiatry of a new medical school at the University of South Florida. Due to the media coverage around the new school, Hollis' mother recognized me and suggested to Hollis that we get together.

Hollis had heard a lot of stories that I did not know about our father. He also knew the rest of the extended family, having for the most part remained in one location while he was growing up. We found the business card of Franz Afeld, who sold artificial flowers in New York City, and knew that he was our great grandfather. We also knew that he was in America around 1865. Like me, Hollis held a firm belief that our family was Jewish.

We shared what we knew – or believed – with a genealogist and from there our exploration began. Over the course of a year, new ancestors and documents emerged and our story began to take shape. At one meeting, I remember the genealogist came to the house with the research that had been conducted in Germany and said, "I've got bad news for your brother. It's Catholics all the way back to at least 1700" - an interesting final joke on us all.

With this journey, I have a fuller feeling now and feel comfortable about my ancestry. I am German and Irish. For the longest time, I felt Irish. My son feels Irish. My daughter feels French, which is interesting. Anyway, I hope that future generations who explore these stories are able to see something of themselves in one of our ancestors. I lived the American Dream and succeeded. I imagine that Franz Afeld, who migrated from Fulda, Germany to New York, seeking a better life and opportunity, would be proud of his legacy – our family.

Walter Edward Afield, M.D.
September 2014

Chapter 1

My Story: by Walter Edward Afield, M.D.

January 1, 2014

At age 78, I wonder about my diverse family background. From whence and from whom did I come?

I was born in 1935 in New York City's now non-existent St. Anne's Hospital, at Madison and Lexington. My mother "Molly" Evelyn McGovern was from Ballymote, County Sligo, Ireland. Much of her background, from the Egans and McGoverns, I knew. Ballymote was a town of 600 people with a ruined 4th century fort and a 6th century abbey. The town is famous for the *Book of Ballymote*, which was written in 1390. We were fortunate to see it locked away in the Royal Irish Academy Archives. It predated the famous "Book of Kells."

My mother was one of 12 children. They were "the social people in town". Her father was a "Victualizers", a butcher - and farm owner who provided the food for the surrounding area. Her father, James, died and her mother, Margaret Egan (seen here in the photo) married his brother, following the cultural tradition of the time.

My mother had problems with men. Everyone was illiterate. My guess is she may well have been abused by her alcoholic stepfather. She described all men as "having bushy beards, dirty, ugly and drunkards". Yet, she described a wonderful, idyllic childhood. She sang all the time and played constantly in the fields of the areas. She used to ride a pony and trap out to

Rosecrib House, the local "mansion" which was the Egan farm, subsequently bought by my Uncle Paddy when he went back to Ireland from America in 1947. It is not much of a house, but it is a lot bigger than the small row houses of Ballymote.

The McGovern's were highly respected in the area. They had their own church pew. Cannon Quinn, described as a nasty rigid autocrat, was the pastor. Mother had only negative things to say about him. Even to this day, his grave on

Rosecrib House in Ballymote, Ireland.

the Church grounds is often desecrated with graffiti. "The Irish forgive, but never forget" my mother was wont to say.

When World War I came, the McGovern boys went off to join the troops to fight the "war with the Huns." The English confiscated all the farms to feed the troops. Margaret was left with all the girls. Uncle Patrick, "Paddy", who was redheaded and reportedly a good singer, went off to join in the battle too. Mrs. Egan, my grandmother's mother, died. Grandfather Egan remarried and had two boys. In those days, boys would inherit the farm and the estate. Women would get nothing. Margaret found herself in desperate straits with no money coming in. She remembered her father saying "If you take those children out of this country, you will never get a thing, and I will never speak to you again", an empty threat since he wasn't giving her any money, anyway. To survive, she left with the children for Glasgow, Scotland, where they grew up in "The Closes", the Catholic slums. At the time, Catholics were often subjected to prejudice. My mother was not allowed in local schools, and, as a result, only had a few years of education. She deeply missed Ireland. Mother went to work in a golf ball factory at eleven pence a week. She did not hold the job long because she threw golf balls out the window to various friends.

Everyone commented on Mother's wonderful voice. One day, sitting on the dock, she was singing "The Last Rose of Summer", a popular English ballad at the time. Someone in the theatre heard her and she was asked to audition at the largest theater in Glasgow. There were three streets that made a U-turn, Bucky Hall, Suckyhall, and Argyle-the old saying was "up Bucky, down Sucky and across Argyle". I believe the theater was on Argyle and was still there when we visited in 1975. My mother auditioned and was an instant star. At 11, my mother was making 15 pounds a week and was supporting the whole family. Subsequently, I found out her mother never attended her performances because that is where "painted ladies were". They were ashamed of her, but gladly took the money. My mother would come onstage in Scottish attire and sing Scottish and English ballads. She was immediately taken on tour of Scotland and England. She performed with Harry Lauder, a well known Scottish vaudevillian, and she was on her way to being a major vaudeville star, still supporting everybody from her salary. Harry Lauder, later to become Sir Harry, took her under his wing and she sang with him: "My Sweet Little Alice Blue Gown", "Just a Wee Deoch an Doris", "There was a Wee Hoose", "Mang the Heather", "The Last Rose of Summer", "Molly Malone" and others.

Uncle Paddy came back from the War and often talked about how, while marching off to the battlefield, he would hear the magnificent music, the drums and the bagpipes playing all the "tunes of glory." "It made the blood boil," he would say. Suddenly, the band would back off, and there would be a "deadening silence." Troops entered the trenches and the endless shooting began. As Paddy described it, he remembered some "giant German with a large mustache and a pointed helmet" coming over the top of the trench pointing his gun and bayonet at him. Paddy shot and killed him and the man fell on him! Paddy vomited! He was subsequently taken prisoner by the Germans. He had great respect for them, because they taught him to read and write.

At the end of the War, he came back to Ireland becoming part of the Irish Republican Army as they fought for independence from England.

The Black and Tans were constantly after him. These were the British recruits who were infamous for their attacks on civilians and civilian property. Their name derived from the improvised khaki uniforms and the dark green or blue police surplus tunics, caps and belts. Paddy was chased by them throughout Ireland. He would stay in the caves around Ballymote and stay hidden in peoples' farm houses. In Belfast, there was a large statue of Oliver Cromwell (known as King Billy) astride a horse. Cromwell was the bane of Catholic existence. Paddy painted the statue with horse manure, put "the bucket of shit" on the tail with a sign saying "Keep your eye on the bucket. I've not finished with him yet". With a price on his head, he was tired of running and left for America. He started a butcher shop in Chicago.

Paddy McGovern at Rosecrib House about 1948.

As a consequence, the women followed. My mother did not. She had a brother, Peter, who lived in Tubbrecurry and ran a butcher shop, never married, and died there. One of the girls became a nurse in England. She returned to Ireland and was a family nurse for a grand Irish family and raised their boy, currently Sir Robert Goff. She is buried with Paddy and his wife Maisie in Ballymote. The others all went to America. They insisted my mother come, and at 18, giving up her rather booming vaudeville career, she left for Chicago. I have a telegram from Harry Lauder telling her not to go. She got to Chicago. It took her a few months to realize this was not the life she wanted.

She went to New York, stayed at the Barbizon Hotel for Women, and got back into show business. She was on what was called the Keith Circuit, which traveled throughout New York, New Jersey and New England, the Keith Memorial Theatre in Boston and the Union Square Theatre and the Capitol Theatre in New York. She was a strikingly beautiful woman. At this point, the vaudevillians were all beginning to get pulled into the "talking movie business". On the circuit, she was with Jack Benny and

Mary. She thought Jack could not play the violin very well and Mary was cold. The Marx brothers, she knew well. Groucho especially. One night on a "date", Groucho took her to a hospital morgue. An autopsy was going on. He was eating a sandwich. My mother ran out yelling at the sight of blood. She said he was a bit strange, but a good jokester. She did like him. Jimmy Durante, she liked a lot. He was under a show business contract to Waxey Gordon, a Philadelphia gangster involved with Arnold Rothstein, Lucky Luciano and Meyer Lansky, notorious gangsters during prohibition. He was trying to get my mother under contract as well as marry her. She remembered his multiple mansions in New York. Attorney General Thomas Dewey was the cause of his 1933 downfall. In 1951 he was put in Alcatraz where he died in 1952. I remember seeing him-short, balding with glasses. My mother was performing at all the local sheik clubs and theaters, such as the Palace Theater. She was a regular at Club 21, a speakeasy where show people and gangsters often mixed. She was a major success. Had she stayed in the business, she would have gone on to Hollywood with all the rest.

Evelyn "Molly" McGovern.

At the Copacabana, a very "in" night spot for the 1920's, she met my father, a good looking charismatic traveling salesman. She did not know that he was married. My mother dated him, married him in Elkton, Maryland, at the time the one-day marriage capital of the world. She got pregnant, and he wanted her to have an abortion. She almost did, but told me she ran out of the doctor's office when she heard the women screaming. Jimmy Durante was my godfather. People tell me they stayed in Greenwich Village for awhile in what colleagues described as a very nice, large townhouse facing the Washington Square Monument. Everything inside was "white". Colleagues remember saying my father would come home to visit. My mother would be very cold towards him. She was very warm towards her friends and toward me, very affectionate. She dedicated her life to me. She gave up her show business career. She had a fair amount of money at this time. She still had friends in the business-Steve Evans, a vaudeville comedian, quite good, looking like Red Skelton, a beginning movie star at the time.

My mother finally discovered her husband had been married and had a son, Hollis, living in New Jersey. He told her he was divorced (which he was not). My mother and I would go to Miami during the winter and stay at the Tides Hotel in South Beach. That was about it for Miami Beach. My father would occasionally visit. I remember his bringing a small radio and we listened, in June of 1941 to the Joe Lewis/Billy Conn heavy weight boxing fight. Billy Conn was very fast on his feet, a former light weight champion. He stayed away from Joe Lewis, "the brown bomber". But then he decided at the end to

Molly McGovern and Walter Afield.

slug it out with him and lost the match. It was one of the great fights and it peaked my interest in boxing. I remember when the Japanese bombed Pearl Harbor. I would go out on the beach in front of the Tides and look up in the air, watching for the Japanese planes. Miami in the winter was a very small town. Driving to Fort Lauderdale was on a dirt road, and we only went there to see a Seminole Indian Village. The Rooney Plaza, now destroyed, was the far northern reach of South Beach and there was nothing beyond.

In the summer, we returned to Elizabeth, New Jersey. We had an apartment at One Dewitt Place. I remember Uncle Paddy coming to visit us there. I remember looking out at him from my crib. I remember one night coming home with my mother and father. All the lights had been turned off, and I was crying. My father had not paid the bill! Obviously, he was having hard times, especially leading a double life married to Hollis's mother who lived with her parents and was supported by them and married to my mother. He took my mother and I to a New Jersey orphanage where he wanted to place me and have her go on the road with him. She put her foot down and said "No". I remember it well!

Walter in front of One Dewitt Place in 1938.

We started the first grade at a place called Pingery Private School in Elizabeth. I finished the first grade in Miami where all they did was make clay models and maybe count from one to 100. When I came back in the spring, Pingery told my mother I could not be promoted because I could not read. My mother, with her limited education and probable dyslexia, would spend summers in upstate New York at Sylvan Beach on Lake Oneida near Utica. She felt the countryside was similar to Ireland, and it gave her comfort. She would go there for the few weeks in the summer where she met the Boolas family. Unas Boolas had come from Lebanon. Mamie was Irish. They married, lived with Mamie's 2 sisters, Jennie and Coey. They never had children. My mother and they hit it off and became lifelong friends and quite important parent figures to me.

That summer, my mother taught me to read. I remember the town, very small and very quiet. Vendor trucks would deliver ice by the block, and we would put it in the top of ice boxes. There was a small carnival in town all the time. We stayed in a hotel on Oneida Beach. There I learned to fish and row a boat, make bonfires on the beach

Mamie and Unas Boolas in 1960.

and roast marshmallows and hot dogs. There was a movie made by a young Liza Minnelli, "The Sterile Cuckoo". The filming took place in Sylvan Beach. One section showed the now destroyed hotel where we stayed.

My mother and I returned to New York. Being suddenly poor, we stayed in a one bedroom apartment on 40th Street, in Queens and lived in an Irish/German neighborhood. The subway stop at Lowery Street ran by our apartment. Day and night-the noise became our clock. I went to P.S. 150, a local grammar school. I was not a spectacular student, but decent. My mother was very lonely, looking all day out a window through a fire escape. Often she would say "Let's go downtown" and get out of "jail" as she called it. We would take the day off and go down to the City: Central Park, the Automat, St. Patrick's Cathedral and Radio City Music Hall. All the first-run movies in the country started at Radio City. There was then the accompanying stage and musical show with the Rockettes. I remember soloists Leonard Warren and Richard Tucker who later became two of the world's greatest opera singers. In grammar school, I have very happy memories of going to the Metropolitan Museum of Art and the Museum of Natural History.

The Police Athletic League took the poor kids to Yankee and Dodgers games and also hockey games. I became "street smart". I always say I got my M.B.A. when I strayed into the Italian neighborhood on 39th Street. There I got my nose broken. I never had it fixed because we could not afford seeing doctors. I did severely cut my right index finger once. A few days later, we went to New York Hospital where a resident saw me. It was too late to do any tendon repair. I realized what it was like to be poor, which we truly were. We knew nothing about how the world worked. The radio constantly informed us of the progress of the War: H.V. Kaltenborn, Walter Winchell, Fulton Lewis, and Lowell Thomas-the commentators for news from the front. In the fifth grade my teacher was overtly a communist. She would constantly talk about Russia and Stalin and how wonderful it would be to live there. The Jewish PM-a communist rag-was her Bible. I would tell my mother and she would be furious. By the time I got to sixth grade, I had developed a deep interest in music. I listened to music at about the age of four-the statutory Rossini Overture to William Tell (the Lone Ranger), Traumeri, Humoresque, Toscanini and the NBC Symphony weekly radio broadcasts from Carnegie Hall. I wanted to take piano lessons. My mother said we could not afford it! Had we, my life might have changed.

Playing on the sidewalk-stick hockey on roller skates, playing imaginary sword fighting, war games, coming home at 5:00PM, reading my comic books, and listening to my stories-"The Shadow", "Spy Smasher". "Terry and the Pirates", "Captain America", "The Lone Ranger"-that was the evening. When I would get sick, doctors would make five dollar house calls with their black bags and full wallets, which my mother pointed out to me. In New Jersey, my mother saw a doctor getting out of residency, a Dr. Wuester. She saw him buy a house and she said "Doctors make money. You've got to be a doctor."

We spent one year at One Dewitt Place in Elizabeth, New Jersey. It was very nice. My Aunt Josephine came from the City and often visited us there. She lived in New York, was not too bright, was a coat check girl at Loew's State Theatre. She was very religious, very Catholic and a caring simple soul. I became an altar boy. This was something one did not do unless one went to Catholic school. "I was in public school" spoketh the nun! On hearing my request the nun in charge laughingly gave me a book of Latin to learn. She didn't think I could. I did in one day and became an altar boy from second grade on all the way to through high school.

The days were filled with stick ball, go carts made out of orange crates and skates, and roller skating on the streets. We would do our ice skating at Flushing Meadows. When the United Nations was formed, they came and took it over as temporary quarters. They threw us all out. We hated them. We used to ice skate on the ponds in Central Park and always ice skated at Rockefeller Center. I became rather good at it. By the time I had gotten to sixth grade, they had administered something called an IQ test. When the teacher left the room, we all went and looked in her grade book to see what she thought of us. My IQ was the highest in the class-164. I did not know what that meant other than it must be bad. The teacher came back to the room, and several of the classmates said "what is this 164 that Afield has?" She said "we just expect 64% more work out of those kinds of people" and made it out to be some sort of disgrace. However, I was placed on a path to skip seventh grade at P.S. 125 and go on to eighth grade and then Stuyvesant High School, the main city public school-feeder to the Ivy League and beyond.

During this time, my father would come home on intermittent weekends, spending the rest of the time "on the road", selling whatever he could sell-sport clothes, perfume, nylon stockings (a rarity during the War). He was very much like Willy Loman in Arthur Miller's "Death of a Salesman". If you read or see the play, you can appreciate the car, the bags, and his personality. "The world depends on a shoeshine and a smile. When they stop smiling, the world collapses". He always said "some day our boat will sail in". I thought this comparable to the warships that would dock in New York and invite visitors. I envisioned a large ship with Afield written on it. It cheered us up. He was good at that! We lived in a one bedroom apartment. I slept on a couch. Everything was concrete in the front and back-our "play yard". The movies, the Bliss Theater, which has now become a Jehovah's Witness center, we would go to all the time. Nine cents to see an afternoon of wonder. We would see a double header, the news, two cartoons and a weekly adventure serial-a big deal at the center of all social life. I remember sitting through King Kong-twice!! The Roxy Theater on Queensborough Boulevard was big time for us. My mother had to come down and get me to come out. We could walk the streets and be safe.

President Franklin Roosevelt was riding down Queensborough Boulevard as he was to address the U.N.. We all went out to see him. I could not have been more than 15 feet away from him while he was in a black convertible and was driving by waving at the people. War Bonds were often sold at rallies in Times Square. My mother and I went one day where Eleanor Roosevelt was the guest, but more importantly for me was Roy Rogers, the "King of the Cowboys". My mother conned the Irish cop at the barricades for me to go up and say hello. I ran up and said "Hi there, Roy Rogers". He turned with Mrs. Roosevelt and said "Hi there, young fella" and Mrs. Roosevelt shook my hand. I was so embarrassed, and I ran back. My mother was angry that she arranged it, and I never followed through.

We used to go to the Automat to eat-put our nickel in a slot, a window would open and a sandwich would come out. A giant silver lions head was on the wall. If you pulled the lever, milk came out of its mouth. We would go to Lindy's for cheesecake. Often we went to Sardi's, and she would show me the show people's wall portraits. I saw all her show business haunts-even St. Malachy's Catholic Church for "show people". Karl Wentz was a German friend and neighbor with his wife and teenage daughter. He was the chief maitre'd at Luchow's, a famous German restaurant, which did not close until the 80's. He often brought home wonderful German foods and desserts. All of us would sit down to the feast of the "hoi poiloy". Karl even wrote a book in German on being a European maitre'd.

It was a happy time for me, but my mother was very sad. All she did was look out a window at a fire escape and again felt she was in jail. When I was 11, my father and mother and I went to Washington to visit the monuments. Alone in the hotel, she told me in hushed tones about the abortion she almost had. She also told me, in hushed tones, that I had a brother by the name of Hollis. "We never talk about him". At eleven, I had no idea what this was all about. It was a bit of a surprise and supposedly a big secret. I think she told me then because she was so depressed. We went to see the Broadway show, "Finian's Rainbow" with Ella Logan, with whom she grew up in Scotland. I could see my mother missed very much not being on the stage and doing that role, which she well would have gotten had she stayed in the business. She had a far better voice, natural, beautiful with full throated projection. In addition, as I said, she was quite a beautiful woman. She saw what she had missed by having me and I think it bothered her.

Since my father was not coming home much, my mother pushed to get back to Florida. She badly wanted it. After a lot of bickering, my father said that we should go to St. Petersburg. We had never heard of it. We knew only Miami. Subsequently, we found out that his parents had died in Clearwater and he had a brother, Robert, who lived and died there in Gulfport. Why did he recommend St. Petersburg? To get us away from Hollis and family. My father's sister also visited Gulfport. Yet, we came. I remember at New York's Grand Central Station saying goodbye to him. My mother was crying. Then it was over. We took the Silver Meteor train to downtown St. Petersburg. We arrived at an old white wooden structure in the middle of town. There were "colored" and "white" waiting rooms and drinking fountains. My first exposure to the south!

We rented a furnished apartment, 727 7th Avenue North. It had one bedroom with two beds, a living room with an oil heater and a very small kitchen, but a big backyard full of fruit trees. A street car came frequently down the front of the street, but at night all was silent. We missed the every 20 minute subway. The landlord, a fine Southern gentleman named Ethridge Rawl, had fallen out of a tree and was crippled. Yet he could ride a three wheel bicycle and used a cane. He used to take me on rides in the car. I learned to ride a bike as together we would go to the beach and everywhere else. In St. Petersburg, the beach was an empty place except for the Don Cesar Hotel at Pass a Grille Beach. For me, he was another important father figure.

My mother made friends with Rose Hurley, another upstate New York Irish woman, who" had a lot of money", at least from our perspective. I think her brother was a Bishop and maybe had been President of University of Notre Dame. Her niece, Rosemary Finnegan, part Philipino, part white went to Columbia, taught at St. Petersburg High School and lived with her aunt. Rosemary introduced me to "Hamlet", Ibsen and Verdi's "La Traviata" on the "new" long playing record. Rose had a car which she would let us use during the summer when she went north. That way we got to drive around and see the city and much of Florida. We lived in a rundown but gorgeous neighborhood, Banyan trees, vines to swing on, two lakes-Round Lake and Mirror Lake up the street. My game playing changed from street games and fighting to biking, swimming, fishing in a small, safe city.

Most of my time was spent in an Andrew Carnegie library at Mirror Lake. I met the Librarian and learned from her what I should read at my age. She gave me all of Hugo, Verne, de Maupassant, Dickens, Walter Scott, Edgar Allen Poe and Hawthorne. The librarian saw something in me and pushed me to read advanced work for the pure joy and adventure. I spent hours in the library as it was air conditioned-one of two such buildings in St. Petersburg. I browsed the stacks and read periodicals. My mother enrolled me in Mirror Lake Junior High and told them of the New York plans for me to skip 7th grade. The Principal said "let us see how he does". I did poorly in the seventh grade. The children in Florida were better educated. They knew grammar. I knew nothing-a typical product of the influence of Columbia University's School of Education, where students should teach themselves and be "free to explore". All schools in New York bought into that disaster. As a consequence the students were behind. Soon that approach was dropped and I stayed in seventh grade.

By the time I got to eighth grade, I took off. I kept talking about wanting to be a doctor, as did my mother. We were figuring out how one gets to be a doctor. Said Rosemary "You go to college-How do you get to college?-You get a scholarship.-How do you get a scholarship?-You get good grades." The message from Rosemary and Rose Hurley stuck. From eighth grade on, it was all A's. Ninth grade was at Mirror Lake and then on to St. Petersburg High School-10th, 11th, and 12th grades.

From there, I applied to college. In those days, all the Ivy League schools were rather provincial and very waspy. In 1953 the SAT's were so new that my total score of 1200 was regarded as "through the roof". I applied but did not know anything about college. I was turned down at Yale and Princeton, accepted at Harvard, MIT, the University of Pennsylvania, Duke, Emory and the Naval Academy. Columbia had the gall to write me and tell me that I was not college material. The University of

Pennsylvania is the only one that offered me a scholarship for tuition, a rarity in those days. Thus, that is where my mother and I went.

My mother followed me to Philadelphia, then pretty much a slum. Urban renewal did not start until 1956. My mother reminisced about leaving Ireland to go to Glasgow. My father thought Penn a good idea because we would be "nearby". He rented us an apartment on campus-absolutely horrible, straw beds! My mother went out and got us a place on 39th and Sansom Street. We were poor. My father gave me some winter clothes that were just awful and obviously hand me downs-over large with a lot of fur necklines. The shoes were too big and he told me to "stick paper in them". He was obviously having a hard time making it. My mother had a small diamond cross that she would pawn to get me warm clothes. Then she would redeem it later. My daughter wears it today. In the Ivy League setting I never had a suit, coat or tie-just samples of his loud Hawaiian shirts. I felt very much out of place and was much derided.

However, I started getting all A's. Those who had gone to private schools were not. One, who was very smart and I saw as a threat, failed out first semester. I remember a young faculty member, Dr. Digby Baltzell, who was just beginning his sociology career. He became famous, coining the terms "wasp" and "preppy" and was world renowned. After he gave us our final exam and I got 100, the only one in the class, he came up and said "Where did you prep?" I did not know what he was talking about. He had to explain to me "Where did you go to high school?" and I told him St. Petersburg High. He was so shocked; he just sort of turned around and said nothing. So much for the "great sociologist" in his first experience with people from other parts of his world, especially the South.

All I did was work at Penn. Since I could type and do short hand (self taught), I worked part time at a job in the Veterinary School library, and in the University Rare Book library. I waited on tables. At one point, I took a job taking daily care of dogs in the Veterinary School, cleaning tons of dog poop. I would wear boots, overalls and carry a big hose and clean the cages. I would flush the feces onto the floor and hose it down the drain. That was the job. A dollar an hour was big money. We continued getting $25 a week from my father which I suppose is equivalent to $250 a week today, still at the poverty line.

Walter at age 20, University of Pennsylvania, where he was a member of the Fencing team.

At the University of Pennsylvania I managed to get through in three years with no summer school-a feat unheard of at the time. All the while, I was working and trying to save money. In high school, I was writing essays and won contests, even national contests. One on medicine, "Why socialized medicine was not good for the United States", won me the national prize of $1000. My mother told me to always put the money aside because my father "would steal it". Thus, we never told him that I was working. In college, all I did was work. I was embarrassed having my mother there. I made no friends, never had a beer, never went to a football game, and had no college life whatsoever. Penn was not an eye opener for me. It was just a place to work. I was also on the fencing team at that time, had a good time with it and wound up doing very well in that sport. That is one of the few things that I did enjoy in college. I also enjoyed a course on Shakespeare. That was about it. The rest was all science. Chemistry, Biology, and Math were my majors.

I had heard about various medical schools and still wanted to be a doctor. I knew Penn was the country's oldest medical school. I had heard about Johns Hopkins after reading a novel, "Miss Suzy Slagles". It was about students who were living in a rooming house and going to Johns Hopkins at the time of its inception. I applied to a variety of medical schools in great secrecy because one "did not" do that. Since computers were invented at Penn, we were registering for courses by computer. All I had to do was walk around a large auditorium with tables and signs telling the subjects. I would pick up punch hole computer cards and turn them in. Yearly I picked up more than the usual 16 credits, usually 18-21 per semester. In one semester I registered for 27 credits. Physical Chemistry, Calculus, French, German, American philosophy which was a requirement, and Advanced Organic Chemistry and Physics. I do not know how I did it!

Anyway, I applied to all these medical schools. My first interview was at the University of Virginia. I went there for the visit. It was fall and gorgeous in Charlottesville. I was impressed. I went down by train and, much to my surprise, one of the interviewers said, "Well, you are going to get into medical school and you should come here." I did not quite resister with that. Three weeks later I was offered a position and immediately accepted it. I went back to Philadelphia and then got called for an interview at Johns Hopkins. I had no real idea what Johns Hopkins was, but I took the train down to Baltimore.

The School and Hospital were right in the middle of the slums with all the original buildings intact and in use. I was interviewed by a group of people. Dean Dr. Phillip Bard, a world renowned physiologist, internist Carmichael Tilghman, and a few other biochemists and surgeon, Alfred Blalock (the world's first heart surgeon). I was fairly cocky in the interview because I had already been accepted at the University of Virginia and was going to go there. We talked about science, chemistry, my interests. I was so self assured. Two days later, I got a letter of acceptance. I was shocked! That doesn't happen that fast! Interestingly, as a rare three year graduate, I was turned down at Penn and all Philadelphia medical schools-Jefferson and Hahnemann. These are the only ones I applied to. Duke and Emory turned me down-Hopkins and UVA saw the light and accepted me. I remember one of my father's very rare visits at that time.

Mother and I told him about Johns Hopkins. For the first time, I think, he was proud of me. He said "You have to go to Johns Hopkins". I told him I had to get my own microscope at $200, a used one, somehow. He came up with the money. I remember everyone at Penn was saying "Don't go to Hopkins. It's not what it used to be". Only Victor Heilbrun, a professor of Mammalian physiology, and his wife, had me to their Rittenhouse Square apartment for dinner. I had never had that experience of dinner in a nice home in what was a major high class neighborhood. During dinner he said Hopkins started in 1893. "Hopkins was the star that shown brightly and changed medical education throughout the world." "Yes, things have changed. It has gotten older and there is another generation in charge. However, Hopkins is still Hopkins." That did it for me!

In the course of college, I did note in the back of my father's car, a letter to a Jeanette Garrette Afield in Brigantine, New Jersey, near the Boardwalk where I spent time as a child. My mother and I got on the train and went to Brigantine. Lo and behold, there was the Jeanette Garrette Dance Studio and a house on the water with the sign Mr. and Mrs. Walter Afield. It turns out, when he divorced his first wife, he never divorced my mother, and married Jeannette Garrette. We were in a state of shock!

I was working that summer at Atlantic Refining, making the enormous sum of $348 a month doing research on rubberized asphalt for roads. That was a big deal. My mother and I lived weekly from check to check from my father. Over the years when the check would come late, we figured he was hurt or he was dead. The only address we had was P.O. Box 333 in Passaic, New Jersey. We did not know how to reach him or anything else. That July there was an announcement in the Philadelphia Enquirer "Walter Afield dies at the Normandy Hotel in San Juan, Puerto Rico." That was after the checks had stopped coming for two weeks. We instinctively knew what had happened and this confirmed it. A major tragedy presented.

The last time I met with him, he was telling me about how to be a doctor and was very proud that I was going to Johns Hopkins. I subsequently found out he even went down to Hopkins, met the Dean, telling them that I was coming there, and sort of being a big shot, as was his wont. When I found out about this many years later from one of the secretaries, I was embarrassed.

When I found out about my father's death, I called the Jeanette Garrette Studio and said that I was a friend of Mr. Afield, and I understood he died. They gave me the address of the funeral parlor. I called the parlor and said that I was his son. At that point, they put Hollis on the phone. Hollis had never heard of me and was in a state of disbelief! I told him I was Walter Afield's son,

Walter in January 1970 as Professor of Psychiatry at Johns Hopkins University Medical School.

Walter, and asked when the funeral was going to be. I wanted to come. He told me when it was. Unfortunately, I could not afford to go. I had to continue working. I remember one day just going in a side room in the Atlantic Refinery Lab and crying. The only time I cried after his death. Only recently have I come to terms about my feelings for him. He did his duty and did the best he could. Obviously he had problems, but he was a bad father for me.

Once he died, my mother said "we cannot afford to go to medical school, it is over". She pushed for me to get my PhD in Chemistry at the University of Pennsylvania. I had applied and been immediately accepted. Still, I said we are going to Hopkins no matter what. I was going to be a doctor. That is what I wanted since I was age four. I stood firm. It was on to Hopkins for us. The Boolas family encouraged me on and even promised money if I needed it. My mother was to come with me. She took the train down to Baltimore, found us a furnished, non-air conditioned apartment in the top floor of some doctor's house-$75 a month. I continued to work at Atlantic Refining.

I remember going to Baltimore by train, dressed in my khaki pants and white t-shirt, carrying a cardboard box with all my belongings tied with ropes. I did not have a suitcase. There was some young preppy passenger, my age, in a seersucker suit and a skimmer hat, sort of looking down his nose at me as if I were some piece of trash. I guess I looked that way. As we got near Baltimore on the train we passed Hopkin's hospital. Some woman pointed out "That's Johns Hopkins" and I said, in a loud voice, "Yes, I am starting there in medical school next week"-so much for Mr. Preppy Asshole across the aisle!

I settled in and immediately went to see Dr. Tilghman, the Associate Dean at the time. I told him my father had died. I had no money. Medical School did not give scholarships in those days. Tilghman gave me a $1000 scholarship and a job. I was to work at Union Memorial Hospital in the Pathology lab. Because of the grueling Medical School curriculum, you were not supposed to work at any outside job. I did. I was running the urine and blood specimens on the weekends. Subsequently, I was doing autopsies for the pathologist who really didn't want to get his hands dirty. Twenty five dollars a body was big time. For more money, monthly I donated blood-$50 a pint for my rare B negative. My mother tried to work. She was uneducated, could not type, much less write. She tried to get a job in a kitchen and got sick. I told her she had to stop. I would support us. Subsequently, I heard many, many years later from one of the secretaries, with whom I was friendly that, Dr. Tilghman said what "Walter Afield is doing the impossible. He is truly a unique and noble man." Starting medical school, I did not realize it was for the rich only. Only later at my 50th class reunion did I learn that. Nobody was poor-everyone was a doctor's son or somebody prominent. I had few friends at Hopkins. I worked. It was a small class-80 people, described as "only the best, the brightest and greatest." I had never had a beer in high school, college or medical school. It was just work, work, work. Much to my surprise I graduated near the top of my class. I wound up going into psychiatry because it was the only specialty where people would talk to patients and show some interest. Likewise, with the election of President Kennedy, it was the "in" thing to do for doctors.

I had been very sophisticated and involved in opera-a huge fan. My mother told me in 1947 that they had Saturday radio broadcasts of live performances of the Metropolitan Opera. I have been listening to it ever since. I was very active in opera. By the time I got to college I knew more than most people. I used to study in the college music room where they had "hi-fi sets". Some of the music students introduced me to Beethoven and some of these other things. As a child I had been regularly listening to the radio broadcasts of Toscanini and the NBC Symphony. I had a natural musical talent and musical interest, but could not carry a tune. There was not much you could do to make a living off of that. New FM radio technology was being tested in New York. WQXR was all classical music. It reached Philadelphia and I was in heaven. I listened all the time. Many of my heroes were opera singers. I subsequently was on the Board of the Boston and Baltimore operas and started an opera company in Florida.

I finally went off to residency at Harvard, which, at that time, was the best residency in the world. I did well there. I wound up being drafted into the U.S. Air Force as was required of us all during the Vietnam War. I was a psychiatrist in Alaska at Elmendorf Air Force Base. Two days after I arrived, there was an earthquake - 8.4 on the Richter scale - the biggest in the world at that time. The whole of what little there was of Anchorage fell apart. The main street was a dirt road. The Air Force's brand new hospital was completely devastated-major cracks everywhere. The hospital commander showed up, lay down on the ground, drunk and cried. We had to air evacuate him to an Air Force Psychiatric hospital in California. Psychiatry was located on the top floor of the new, but ruined hospital. The hierarchy decided to just "plug up all these gashes with some kind of glue". I remember speaking to the new hospital commander about safety issues. Major aftershocks continued for all the years I was there. His retort on safety was "if there is a quake, ride a slab of concrete down to the bottom".

There was not much to do in Anchorage. I went from dating Princess Christina of Sweden (a Harvard student) and a cultural life to a monastic life. It was, however, the first time I really made close friends. It was like being in a college dorm, drinking beer, conversing. No mother with me. It would get dark at about 1:00 in the afternoon and it would get daylight at about 11:00 in the morning during the winter. Temperature was from 80 below to 30 above, outdoor barbecue weather. During the summer, it was daylight all the time. We would all go to "the top of the world", a five-story hotel not devastated by the earthquake to watch the sun pop up and down behind Mt. McKinley, 150 miles away.

Two years later I got out of the service. I was uncertain about the future. I was thinking of going to San Francisco to practice and then decided to go back to Boston. Driving the 2500 mile dirt road, the Alcan Highway, the only way out of Alaska, gave me a lot of time to think. They offered me a child psychiatry position at Harvard's Massachusetts General Hospital. I took it. I was subsequently invited back to Hopkins as an Assistant Professor where I ran child psychiatry for three years.

In 1970, I came to Tampa, Florida as Professor and Chairman of the Department of Psychiatry of a new medical school at the University of South Florida. At the time, my mother was living in St. Petersburg. I remember telling a Hopkins colleague this job offer is very good for a man so young, but it's twenty five miles from my mother. His immediate response-"I wish my mother were alive and only 25 miles away!" I took the job and cared for my mother until her death in 1986. She had rheumatic fever as a child which affected her heart. She needed a cardiac valve replaced. She bought a grave, sent me the bill and

Walter Afield at the future site of the medical school at the University of South Florida in 1970.

survived the surgery. She did see her grandchildren and was very active with them until 10 years later when they had to replace the defective heart valve. She is buried in Sylvan Abbey in Clearwater.

When I moved to Tampa, the medical school was unapproved, uncertified and an empty lot. I was the only clinical doctor there. First, I had to start a mental health hospital, build a 200 bed psychiatric unit at a new, under construction, Veteran Administration Hospital, build a medical school, recruit faculty, get accreditation, start a class, and negotiate teaching agreements with local hospitals. It was wonderful and an extensive administrative experience, but bloodthirsty and highly political. Local doctors did not want the medical school to exist. Too much competition, said they.

After four years of this experience, I was in great demand and offered multiple jobs around the country-one as Dean of Cornell Medical School, one Chairmanship at New York University, one Chairmanship at Stanford and the position of Commissioner of Mental Health in Boston along with a Clinical Professorship at Harvard.

At this point I really had gotten tired of the rat race. I realized that I had been dealing with academia as the lost father figure that I never knew. School became my lost father and the schools I went to pushed everyone into Academia. These were my father figures, but enough was enough. I remember Cornell telling me 'they did not want me for my teaching ability, they wanted me as a "hatchet man" to fire people, get rid of some tenured faculty they could no longer handle, and raise money." I was obviously a builder. That meant if I took that job, I would have to move on. Those jobs were usually short term-four, five, six years. You would have to move and move and move.

My Wife, Nancy Browning

I stayed in Tampa, started a practice, and got married to a wonderful woman-Nancy Browning. Nancy and I have been married 40 years now. My wife's side of the family is easily accessed in the book "Genealogy of the Brownings in America from 1621 to 1908". Her grandfather's name was Henry Prentice Browning, who is the last entry in Nancy's family line in the book (page 303, ancestor number 1038).

Her father was Henry Prentice Browning II. He started his career in Chicago at the Continental Bank, then moved to Worcester,

Massachusetts and then moved to Indianapolis, where he ran the largest bank in the Midwest, American Fletcher National Bank. He went to New York as a bank President at the National Bank of North America. He then retired to Florida where he owned his own bank -- he called it his "piggy bank" -- and did a lot of sailing on his boat out into the Gulf of Mexico. He died in his mid-90's and is buried at Sylvan Abbey in Clearwater, Florida.

Charles Downer Browning

b: 04 Feb 1835 in Stonington, New London, Connecticut
m: 03 Jan 1859 in New London, Connecticut
d: 12 Feb 1899 in Norwich, New London, Connecticut

Henry P. Browning

b: Jul 1871 in Norwich, New London, Connecticut
m: 1899 in Manhattan, New York, USA
d: 07 Jun 1927 in Manhattan, New York

Henrietta Carey Lathrop

b: 23 Jun 1838 in Lebanon, New London, Connecticut
d: 06 Sep 1895 in Norwich, New London, Connecticut

Henry Prentice Browning

b: 01 Jun 1913 in Montclair, Essex, New Jersey
d: 26 May 1994 in Tampa, Hillsborough, Florida

Edward Whittemore Bartow

b: 01 Apr 1841 in Maryland
m: 1868
d: 1899 in Long Beach, Nassau, New York

Ida Stewart Bartow

b: 16 Jul 1872 in New York City
d: 1936

Maria L. Knower

b: Abt. 1845 in New York

Obituary of H. Prentice Browning

H. Prentice Browning, 93, died in his sleep at Canterbury Towers, Tampa, Florida. One of the most prominent bankers of his generation, he was born in Montclair, New Jersey to parents Henry P. Browning and Ida Bartow. After graduating in 1933 from Amherst College, he started his banking career at Continental Bank of Illinois in Chicago. This was interrupted by World War II where he was a lieutenant directing construction of battleships at the San Francisco Navel Yard. Upon discharge he became Vice President of the Worcester County Trust Company in Worcester, Massachusetts. He then went on to become President of American Fletcher National Bank in Indianapolis. There he was involved with the merger with Fidelity Trust Company making it one of the largest banks in the Midwest. He was the first to computerize a bank outside of New York and one of the first in the United States to promote women to officer status. Subsequently, the bank was sold to Bank One. Quite active in Indianapolis, he impacted the community as President of Methodist Hospital, Chairman of the United Way, President of the Board of Trustees of Butler University as well as consultant to multiple civic organizations. As an aside, through friendships with Theodor Geisel (Dr. Seuss) and New York media, he overcame considerable resistance and got, for the first time, "How the Grinch Stole Christmas" on national television. Returning east, he was chairman and CEO of New York City's National Bank of North America. He moved on to Tampa, and assumed the position of CEO and President of the Exchange Bank Corporation, which became NCNB and then Bank of America. In his brief tenure, he brought about innovations in Florida banking, including the introduction of branch banking to the state. He was on the Board of Directors of the University of Tampa and a member of the University Club and Tampa Yacht and Country Club. Retiring, he started his own bank, The Palm State Bank in Palm Harbor subsequently selling it to Bank One. In his retirement during the 80's and 90's, he lived on Anna Maria Island where he continued to mentor younger bankers, many of whom went on to assume national prominence. He remained on the boards of Arvin Industries, The Family Institute in New Orleans and multiple other boards. Throughout his 70's and 80's he engaged in his frequent golf and tennis games and sailing his beloved boat "Peace" throughout Florida waterways. He continued his love of Amherst with an active involvement in the Florida West Coast Amherst Club. At his 60th Amherst Reunion he was recognized for saving from destruction a granite monument which belonged to a beloved retired Latin Professor, Haven D. Brackett. Slated for destruction because the new Massachusetts Turnpike was coming through his property, Mr. Browning had the monument transported to Amherst where it was placed in front of the Alumni House. Engraved on it is a phrase from an ode by Horace, which translated is: "Of all places on this earth this one smiles on me the most."

Enormously successful professionally, he prided himself most on his wife Jane, three children, H. Prentice Browning Jr. (deceased), Penny (Mr.and Mrs. Russell Fortune of Indianapolis) and Nancy (Dr. and Mrs. Walter Afield of Tampa) and his grandchildren, Ted Afield an attorney in Tampa and newly married granddaughter Neva Browning Jeffries and her husband Justin Jeffries, both attorneys in Atlanta. Services are private with internment in Sylvan Abbey in Clearwater.

His wife, Jane Littell, had been the daughter of Guy Littell who had been the CEO of the world's largest publishing house, R.R. Donnelley in Chicago. Guy Littell hated the Irish, hated the unions and hated FDR. He was annoyed with his daughter for having Nancy born on FDR's birthday. Jane was induced, so she could have had Nancy on another day. It turns out his family goes all the way back to French Huguenot stock. On my father-in-law's side, his mother's maiden name was Bartow which traces all the way back into early American history with Louise Bartow who married a shipping magnate in New York. It then becomes Bertiaux and traces all the way back to the 1300's when Henri de Navarre was convinced by a Bishop Bertiaux to become Catholic. He subsequently became King of France. As King, he Catholicized all of the country with the phrase "what are a few masses for Paris".

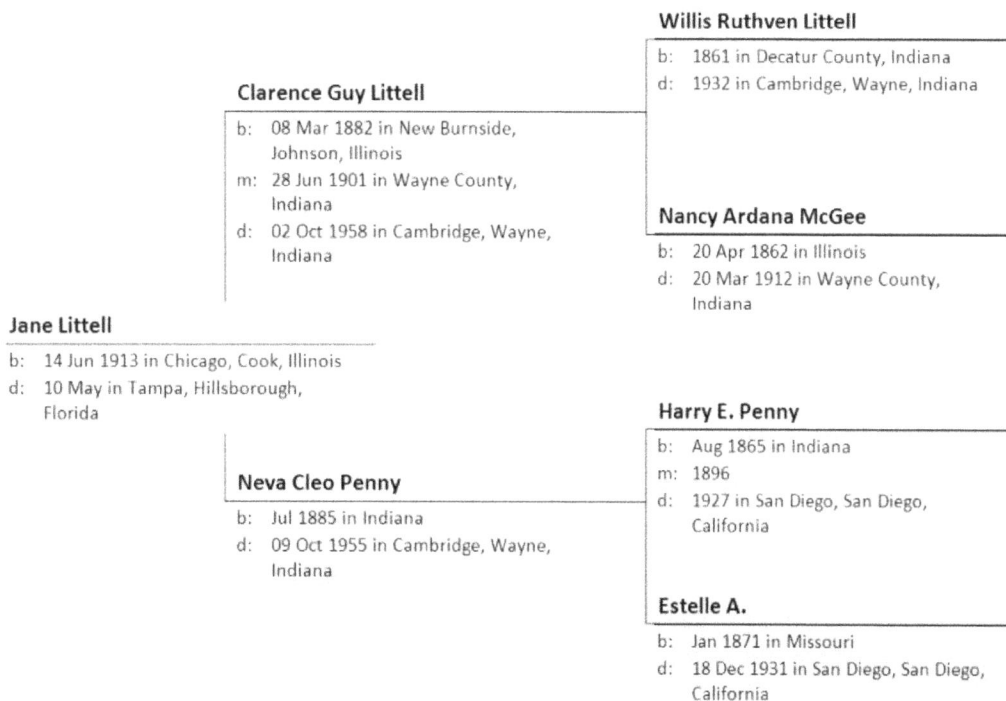

Willis Ruthven Littell

b: 1861 in Decatur County, Indiana
d: 1932 in Cambridge, Wayne, Indiana

Clarence Guy Littell

b: 08 Mar 1882 in New Burnside, Johnson, Illinois
m: 28 Jun 1901 in Wayne County, Indiana
d: 02 Oct 1958 in Cambridge, Wayne, Indiana

Nancy Ardana McGee

b: 20 Apr 1862 in Illinois
d: 20 Mar 1912 in Wayne County, Indiana

Jane Littell

b: 14 Jun 1913 in Chicago, Cook, Illinois
d: 10 May in Tampa, Hillsborough, Florida

Harry E. Penny

b: Aug 1865 in Indiana
m: 1896
d: 1927 in San Diego, San Diego, California

Neva Cleo Penny

b: Jul 1885 in Indiana
d: 09 Oct 1955 in Cambridge, Wayne, Indiana

Estelle A.

b: Jan 1871 in Missouri
d: 18 Dec 1931 in San Diego, San Diego, California

Obituary of Jane Littell

Jane Littell Browning passed away on May 10th, 2008 at Tampa General Hospital. Mrs. Browning was born in Chicago to Clarence Guy Littell and Neva Penny Littell on June 14th, 1913. She grew up in Kenilworth on the North Shore of Chicago. Jane Browning graduated from Pine Manor College in Boston. She then moved back to Kenilworth and was active in the social and the tennis scene. She met her husband, H. Prentice Browning on a blind double date. The only problem was, Prentice was the other girl's date. Adding to the dilemma,

Jane's date and Prentice's date were brother and sister. Jane and Prent danced the night away, while the brother and sister could but watch. Jane and Prent married October 7th, 1939 and were married 65 years until his death in 2005. Jane was a major help in Prentice's career as he moved up the banking ladder from Continental Bank of Illinois to Worcester County Trust Company in Worcester, MA, eventually becoming President of American Fletcher National Bank in Indianapolis, Indiana, (now Chase),New York's National Bank of North America and then Exchange Bank (subsequently Bank of America) of Tampa. Jane was devoted to her husband and her three children: Penny Browning Fortune (husband Russell Fortune III), of Indianapolis, Nancy Browning Afield (husband Dr. Walter E. Afield) of Tampa, Florida and H. Prentice Browning Jr. who passed away in 1994. She also doted on her two grandchildren Walter E. "Ted" Afield, an attorney and soon to be a law professor, and law professor Browning Afield Jeffries (husband Justin Clay Jeffries) of Atlanta, Georgia.

Jane and Prent retired to Anna Maria Island, Florida where they spent wonderful years entertaining friends, sailing, biking and walking the beautiful beaches before both becoming ill at the same time in January of 1998. After recovery, they moved into Canterbury Towers in Tampa, where Jane spent her last 10 years. Her main joys were her children and grandchildren. Her last outing, less than a week before she died, was to go to St. John's Episcopal Church to hear her grandson, Ted, sing Mozart's "Coronation Mass" with the Mendelssohn Choir. She was a magnificent wife and mother, and a loving grandmother. A private person, she was a great friend, never said a bad word about anyone and was a decent, warm and caring person, one whom God will welcome with open arms.

A private graveside service will be held Saturday, May 17th at Sylvan Abbey in Clearwater.

Henry Prentice Browning and his wife, Jane Littell.

Our Children

We had two children-Walter Edward Afield III "Ted" and Neva Browning Afield, using Nancy's maiden name of Browning and her grandmother's name of Neva.

Neva Browning Afield

Neva Browning Afield.

Walter, Nancy, Browning, Justin, and Ted.

Browning would not go to college "north of the Mason Dixon Line". She went to Duke and then went to the University of Virginia Law School, then to Atlanta to practice. She is now a Professor at John Marshall School of Law in Atlanta. She married Justin Jeffries, who was two years ahead of her.

They had both gone to Duke but didn't meet until they both went to UVA Law School. He had worked a few years before law school, so now they were in the same class. He is a lawyer who works for the Securities and Exchange Commission. They have been married nine years and have no children.

Justin, President Jimmy Carter, Rosalynn Carter, Browning.

Walter Edward "Ted" Afield III

Ted went to Harvard, was an international fencer, international singer in choirs, singing all over England, Scotland and France. He went to Columbia Law School. After that, he came back to Florida. He did not wish to stay there and do the rough and tough political climb to be a partner in a large New York Law Firm. He spent some time in the White House in the Office of the General Counsel to President Clinton. He also worked with Vice President Al Gore. He had no plans on expanding this career further.

Ted with Newt Gingrich, who was the 58th Speaker of the U.S. House of Representatives.

He returned to Tampa, practiced for awhile, got a judicial clerkship and got a Masters Degree in tax law-the LLM. He did not like private practice. He is a very moral and devoted Catholic man who decided he was going to go back into academia. However, he did not want to leave Florida.

Walter Edward "Ted" Afield III.

Walter, Nancy, Sarah, Ted, Browning and Justin.

At that time, there was a new law school called Ave Maria which started in Ann Arbor, Michigan and was built by the man who created Domino's Pizza, Tom Monaghan. He felt the Catholic law schools were not Catholic enough, so he created a new one and planned to keep it the most Catholic of all. Ave Maria had been an approved law school. They asked Ted to come up there to give a speech. He liked it, and they liked him. He went there for nine months and then they moved the school to Naples, Florida which is where he is currently a Dean and Tax Professor. He is as happy as he can be.

He married Sarah Murphy, a strong Catholic, who has a sister who is a Dominican Nun and another sister with six children. She is likewise – an attorney. Hopefully, there will be grandchildren in our future. He is doing a wonderful thing, as is my daughter. We raised two superstar children. It is truly the best thing I ever participated in.

Ted with Governor Jeb Bush, the 43rd Governor of Florida (1999-2007).

Full Circle

For the longest time, I thought my ancestors were Jewish - probably because my father hated Jews. Around 1940 changed his name from Afeld to Afield, adding an "I" because "Afeld sounded too Jewish." In reality, I knew nothing about the family on his side and decided I would research that. I learned a lot more when I began to spend time with Hollis, my half-brother, in the 1970's. I had come back to Tampa to take a position as Professor and Chairman of the Department of Psychiatry of a new medical school at the University of South Florida. Due to the media coverage around the new school, Hollis' mother recognized me and suggested to Hollis that we get together.

Hollis had heard a lot of stories that I did not know about our father. He also knew the rest of the extended family, having for the most part remained in one location while he was growing up. We found the business card of Franz Afeld, who sold artificial flowers in New York City, and knew that he was our great grandfather. We also knew that he was in America around 1865.

We shared what we knew – or believed – with a genealogist and from there our exploration began. Over the course of the next year, new ancestors and documents emerged and our story began to take shape. At one meeting, I remember the genealogist came to the house with the research that had been conducted in Germany and said, "I've got bad news for your brother. It's Catholics all the way back to at least 1700" - an interesting final joke on us all.

With this journey, I have a fuller feeling now and feel comfortable about my ancestry. I am German and Irish. For the longest time, I felt Irish. My son feels Irish. My daughter feels French, which is interesting. Anyway, I hope that future generations who explore these stories are able to see something of themselves in one of our ancestors. I lived the American Dream and succeeded. I imagine that Franz Afeld, who migrated from Fulda, Germany to New York, seeking a better life and opportunity, would be proud of his legacy – our family. I am glad Franz came to New York.

Chapter 2

The Afeld Family of Fulda, Germany

My 4th Great Grandparents
Heinrich Afeld and Maria Magdalena Harner

Heinrich Afeld was born about 1735. He had three sons and two daughters with Maria Magdalena Harner between 1755 and 1775.

Heinrich Afeld			Maria Magdalena Harner	
Born: Abt. 1735			Born: Abt. 1735	
Died: 21 Jul 1784 Fulda, Hesse-Nassau, Germany			Died: 04 Jan 1802 Fulda, Hesse-Nassau, Germany	

Marriage:			
Children:	**Sex**	**Birth**	**Death**
Johannes Afeld	M	Abt. 1755 Fulda, Hesse-Nassau, Germany	Nov 1840 Fulda, Hesse-Nassau, Germany
Maria Anna Afeld	F	23 Aug 1770 Fulda, Hesse-Nassau, Germany	
Joseph Afeld	M	1772 Fulda, Hesse-Nassau, Germany	
Josepha Afeld	F	1774 Fulda, Hesse-Nassau, Germany	
Franz Anton Afeld	M	1775 Fulda, Hesse-Nassau, Germany	

According to research conducted at the Cathedral Archives in Fulda, Germany, the Afeld name began to appear in the records in 1770, with the birth of their daughter, Maria Magdalena. There is no birth record for their oldest son nor is there a marriage record for them, so it is most likely that the family moved to Fulda around 1769. No clues were found pointing toward where the family lived prior.

The records do show that Heinrich was a "street paver," which at the time would mean installing either cobblestone or brick. Heinrich died on July 21, 1784, in Fulda, Germany, at the age of 49. Maria survived Heinrich and died on January 4, 1802, in Fulda.

Translation: 21 [day]. Heinrich Afeld, streetpaver, 49 years of age.

My 3rd Great Grandparents
Johannes Afeld and Maria Catharina Hillenbrand

Johannes Afeld was born about 1755 in Hesse-Nassau, Germany. He married Maria Catharina Hillenbrand on September 7, 1795, the daughter of Paul Hillenbrand and Elisabeth Hagermann, both residents of Fulda.

Translation: September 7 - Johannes Afeld, street paver, a legitimate son of Henirich Afeld and Magdalena Harner, who are married; and Catharina, of the marriage of Paul Hillenbrand and Elisabeth Hagermann. Wittnesses Joseph Knips, butcher, and Adam Wäider, [unknown occupation].

Johannes and Maria had three sons and one daughter between 1797 and 1802.

Johannes Afeld		Maria Catharina Hillenbrand	
Born:	Abt. 1755	Born:	Abt. 1761
	Fulda, Hesse-Nassau, Germany		Fulda, Hesse-Nassau, Germany
Died:	Nov 1840	Died:	10 Nov 1840
	Fulda, Hesse-Nassau, Germany		Fulda, Hesse-Nassau, Germany

Marriage:	07 Sep 1795 in Fulda, Hesse-Nassau, Germany; Source: Marraige Register

Children:	Sex	Birth	Death
Johann Valentin Afeld	M	23 Nov 1797 Fulda, Hesse-Nassau, Germany	
Joseph Adam Afeld	M	03 Aug 1799 Fulda, Hesse-Nassau, Germany	
Adam Joseph Afeld	M	03 Oct 1800 Fulda, Hesse-Nassau, Germany	22 Jan 1851 Fulda, Hesse-Nassau, Germany
Maria Catharina Afeld	F	04 Nov 1802 Fulda, Hesse-Nassau, Germany	

Johannes followed in his fathers' occupation as a street paver.

He died in November 1840 in his hometown, having lived a long life of 85 years. Maria died November 10, 1840 in Fulda. The available image was to faint to print, but the translation of the records follows:

Translation: Entry 1769; District 5; Catharina Afeld, widow of the late paver, Johann Afeld.

My Great Great Grandparents
Adam Joseph Afeld and Anna Maria Drinnenberg

When Adam Joseph Afeld was born on October 3, 1800, in Fulda, Nassau, Germany, his father, Johannes, was 45 and his mother, Maria Catharina, was 39.

Translation: 3 – Adam Joseph Afeld, the legitimate son of John and Catharina Hillenbrand were married by the church. Patron, Adam Joseph Schreiner.

He married Anna Maria Drinnenberg about 1824 and together, they had four sons, four daughters, and one other child who was either still-born or died shortly after birth, between 1825 and 1836.

Adam Joseph Afeld		Anna Maria Drinnenberg	
Born:	03 Oct 1800	Born:	22 Jan 1801
	Fulda, Hesse-Nassau, Germany		Hunfeld, Hesse, Germany
Died:	22 Jan 1851	Died:	06 Jan 1848
	Fulda, Hesse-Nassau, Germany		Fulda, Hesse-Nassau, Germany

Marriage:	27 Apr 1824 in Hünfeld, Fulda, Hesse, Germany

Children:	Sex	Birth	Death
Catharina Josepha Afeld	F	09 Mar 1825 Fulda, Hesse-Nassau, Germany	
Franz Wilhelm Afeld	M	12 Sep 1826 Fulda, Hesse-Nassau, Germany	02 Nov 1904 New York City, New York
Johannes Joseph Afeld	M	17 Feb 1828 Fulda, Hesse-Nassau, Germany	Bef. 1845 Fulda, Hesse-Nassau, Germany
Anna Josepha Afeld	F	31 Mar 1829 Fulda, Hesse-Nassau, Germany	Bef. 1845 Fulda, Hesse-Nassau, Germany
Unnamed Afeld	?	19 Sep 1830 Fulda, Hesse-Nassau, Germany	19 Sep 1830 Fulda, Hesse-Nassau, Germany
Maria Anna Catharina Theresia Afeld	F	18 Dec 1831 Fulda, Hesse-Nassau, Germany	
Benedikt Joseph Afeld	M	20 Oct 1833 Fulda, Hesse-Nassau, Germany	
Elisabeth Afeld	F	12 Mar 1836 Fulda, Hesse-Nassau, Germany	Bef. 1855 Fulda, Hesse-Nassau, Germany
Josef F. Afeld	M	16 Sep 1837 Fulda, Hesse-Nassau, Germany	31 Mar 1903 San Francisco, California

Anna Maria Drinnenberg was born at Hünfeld, a district just outside of Fulda, Germany, on January 22, 1801. Her parents were Johann Phillipe Drinnenberg and Maria Barbara Köhler.

Translation: Hünfeld/Drinnenberg -- On the 22nd of this month is baptized Anna Maria. Phillip Drinnenberg, a shoemaker, and his wife Maria Barbara, by birth a Köhler, a virgin, and the legitimate child of Anna Maria Köhler.

The Cathedral records did provide sufficient documentation to construct the lineage of Anna Maria Drinneberg back some four generations. This information can be found in Chapter 6 - *The Drinneberg Family of Hünfeld, Germany.*

Anna Maria died on January 6, 1848, at age 47 in Fulda and Adam died on January 22, 1851, in his hometown, at the age of 50.

Chapter 3

The Afeld Brothers Come to America: Josef F. AFeld

Josef F. Afeld

Josef was born on September 16, 1837 in Fulda, Hesse-Nassau, Germany, the son of Adam Afeld and Anna Maria Drinnenberg. He immigrated to the United States in 1860. No passenger arrival records were located.

He appeared in Superior Court of New York County and was naturalized on October 10, 1860. When asked about his "former nationality," he replied that his allegiance was to the Duke of Hesse Cassel. (National Archives and Records Administration; Washington, D.C.; Petitions for Naturalizations Filed in Federal, State, and Local Courts in New York City, 1792-1906 (M1674); Microfilm Serial: M1674; Microfilm Roll: 1.)

Josef was engaged in the artificial flower business with his brother and first appears in the New York City Directory in 1861. On July 1, 1863, he registered in the Fourth District, New York, for the Class I part of the Civil War draft registration. There is no indication that he was called to service.

Consolidated Lists of Civil War Draft Registrations, 1863-1865. NM-65, entry 172, 620 volumes. Records of the Provost Marshal General's Bureau (Civil War), Record Group 110. National Archives at Washington D.C.

In 1867, Josef married Elizabeth F., a German who immigrated around 1848 according to census records. No marriage record was located at the Municipal Archives in New York City where a search was conducted between the years 1866 and 1868. No other document was identified that disclosed the maiden name of Elisabeth. We glean from the census and other records that she was born in the broad region known as Bavaria, between 1842 and 1847 and that she immigrated in either 1848 or 1849.

By 1871, Josef left the artificial flower business and opened a musical instruments store located at 355 Bowery Street in New York. The store is listed in the city directories each year through 1875. Sometime between 1875 and 1876, Josef and Elizabeth moved to San Francisco. They would have traveled across the recently completed Transcontinental Railroad, which covered 1,907 miles between Council Bluffs, Iowa and San Francisco. The journey would have taken them about a week, as compared to travel by stagecoach, which would have taken four-to six weeks or longer.

TO CLOSE AT EIGHT.

Success of the Salesmen's Movement.

SHORTER HOURS FOR CLERKS.

A List of the Merchants Who Will Put Up Their Shutters at Eight.

The efforts of the Retail Clerks' Association have met with success, and the early-closing movement begins to-night. The retail business of the city will hereafter cease at 8 o'clock. The Executive Committee of the association has found but little difficulty in convincing employers that the hours of labor were too long, and that trade and profits would be just as satisfactory if buyers were compelled to do their purchasing before a late hour in the evening. A few of the minor firms hold out, but their names will be handed to the Federated Trades and the Knights of Labor for further consideration, and it is expected that the force of example and public opinion will bring them into line with the majority. Following are the names and addresses of the firms that have signed the agreement:

Josef was one of the supporting businesses listed in favor of early closure rules. (San Francisco Chronicle, July 6, 1886, vol. 43 no 173, page 5.)

Life in the American West

While we have no personal written records from Josef, it is clear that he actively participated in his community.

Josef first registered to vote in San Francisco on October 10, 1876. He is then found in the San Francisco City Directory for many years, with his occupation recorded as either "music store" or "merchant." Their residence was at 805 Larkin Street. The ground floor of the building was occupied by the store and they lived on the upper level. Today, the property is a part of Sergeant John Macaulay Park.

Below is an advertisement published in the San Francisco Chronicle for the music store. As Josef made the transition from New York to San Francisco, he appears to have specialized, selling only string instruments. (San Francisco Chronicle April 24, 1891; Vol. 53, No. 99, page 6.)

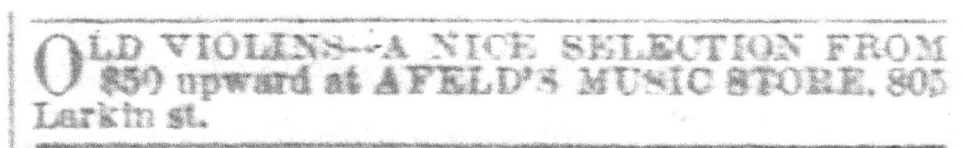

OLD VIOLINS—A NICE SELECTION FROM $50 upward at AFELD'S MUSIC STORE, 805 Larkin st.

What Did Josef Look Like?

While no photos of Josef Afeld were found, we do have a good description of what he looked like. The information captured by voter registration changed from year to year, but Josef's record in 1898 however provides a snapshot of the man. He registered on July 23, 1898, in Precinct 7, Assembly District 39. He is age 63, 5 feet 2 inches tall, has green eyes and brown hair, with a fair complexion and no visible marks or scars. He is a native of Germany and was naturalized in New York Superior Court on October 10, 1860. He read the Constitution, signed his name, and marked his ballot. (California State Library, California History Section; Great Registers, 1866-1898; Collection Number: 4 - 2A; CSL Roll Number: 114; FHL Roll Number: 977275.)

JOSHUA HAMBLIN.

His Fourth Trial for Murder Commenced.

At noon yesterday the impaneling of the jury in the fourth Hamblin murder trial was concluded. The names of the persons are: M. Stockwitz, J. L. Martel, R. E. Cole, Joseph Afeld, J. Anderson, Casper Reichling, John F. Kelly, W. B. Wilshire, C Ferris, F. Franks, John M. Sherbourne, J. Herzog.

Charles B. Smith, the companion of John N. Massey on the night of his murder, was put on the stand and the old story of the crime was rehearsed. George A. Knight is counsel for the defense and the District Attorney is assisted by Henry Edgerton.

Left, on April 26, 1887, Josef was impanelled on a Jury to hear evidence against Josh Hamblin in his fourth murder trial. (San Francisco Chronicle, April 27, 1887, vol. 45 no. 102, page 6.)

Below, on May 6, having failed to reach a verdict, the judge locked them in the jury room all night. (San Francisco Chronicle, May 7, 1887, vol. 45 no. 112, page 6.)

HAMBLIN CONVICTED.

GUILTY OF MANSLAUGHTER.

Verdict of the Jury After a Long Deliberation.

The jury in whose hands was cast the fate of Joshua Hamblin, charged with murder, for shooting and killing John N. Massey, early in the morning of April 2, 1882, did not arrive at a verdict until nearly twenty-eight hours had been consumed in deliberating and balloting. It will be remembered that the case was given to the jury about 11:30 A. M. on Thursday. Not agreeing by 6 P. M., the jurors were locked up for the night in the cold and cheerless jury-room. Judge Toohy had decided that inasmuch as Hamblin had been tried four times, he would keep the jurors out until they either convicted or acquitted the prisoner. During Thursday night the jurors had anything but a pleasant or agreeable time. After they had grown very weary of casting ballots, many sought relaxation by resting their heads on the table and catching brief intervals of sleep. They were liberated from their close quarters at 6:30 o'clock yesterday morning and given a hasty breakfast at the expense of the city, after which they were returned to the jury-room. Several of the jurors were seen to stick their heads out of a window and gaze wistfully at the scenery in Dunbar alley—alluring beer signs.

When Judge Toohy opened court at 10 o'clock Hamblin showed signs of having spent an exceedingly restless night. His faithful attorney, George A. Knight, whispered words of cheer in his ear that made a gleam of hope visible on his countenance. Nothing more was heard from the jurors until 2 P. M., when they entered the courtroom and their foreman announced that they had not yet agreed upon a verdict. Attorney Knight was not present, and Judge Toohy sent them back to their room, promising to bring them back when Knight returned.

At 3 o'clock arguments in the never-ending Hope case were stopped and the jurors were again taken into court. When it was announced that they still disagreed Judge Toohy asked:

"Do you disagree upon propositions of law or facts?"

"Upon questions of facts," responded Foreman Franks.

"Then," said the court, "you must retire again and deliberate until you do agree upon a verdict."

Half an hour later the jurors were again allowed to leave their room.

"Gentlemen of the jury," asked Clerk Desmond, "have you agreed upon a verdict?"

There was a start of surprise among the spectators when Foreman Franks stated "We have."

"Gentlemen of the jury, what is your verdict?"

"We, the jury, find the defendant guilty of manslaughter."

The verdict seemed to have no effect on Hamblin. He remained seated in his chair with cold and emotionless features. No signs of weakness were shown by him when a deputy Sheriff conducted him back to the County Jail, where he has spent five long years.

Judge Toohy set the 14th inst., one week from to-day, as the time for imposing sentence.

In the 1900 US Federal Census, Elizabeth indicated that she had given birth to no children and none were discovered in any other record source. Josef died in 1903 and was interred at the San Francisco Columbarium (Floor 2, Section I).

> **AFELD** – In this city, March 31, Josef, beloved husband of Elisabeth Afeld, and brother of Mrs. John Koeppen of Marion, Ind., and Franz Afeld of New York, a native of Fulda, Kur Hessen, Germany, aged 65 years, 5 months, and 15 days.
>
> Friends and acquaintances are respectfully invited to attend the funeral Thursday, April 2, at 2 o'clock, from the parlors of Theodore Dierks, undertaker, 957 Mission street, between Fifth and Sixth; thence to Odd Fellows's Crematorium for incineration. (San Francisco Chronicle, April 2, 1903, volume 77, number 77, page 12)

Elizabeth Survives the Great San Francisco Earthquake and Fire in 1906

The San Francisco earthquake of 1906 struck San Francisco at 5:12 a.m. on Wednesday, April 18, 1906. Fires broke out in the city that lasted for three days. As a result of the quake and fires, about 3,000 people died and over 80% of San Francisco was destroyed. About 300,000 people were rendered homeless out of a population of about 410,000. Half of those who evacuated fled across the bay to Oakland and Berkeley. Newspaper reports describe Golden Gate Park, the Presidio, and area beaches as covered with makeshift shelters and tents.

The earthquake was the first natural disaster of its magnitude to be documented by photography and motion picture footage. The overall cost of the damage from the earthquake was estimated at the time to be around $400 million or about $9.5 billion in 2014 dollars.

Residents watching the fire from Golden Gate Park. (Photo by Ralph O. Hotz, courtesy of the US Geological Survey Library, Menlo Park, California.)

This photo is a view looking down Geary Street. The Afeld's store and home was one block from this location. (Photo by R. B. Marshall, courtesy of the US Geological Survey Library, Menlo Park, California.)

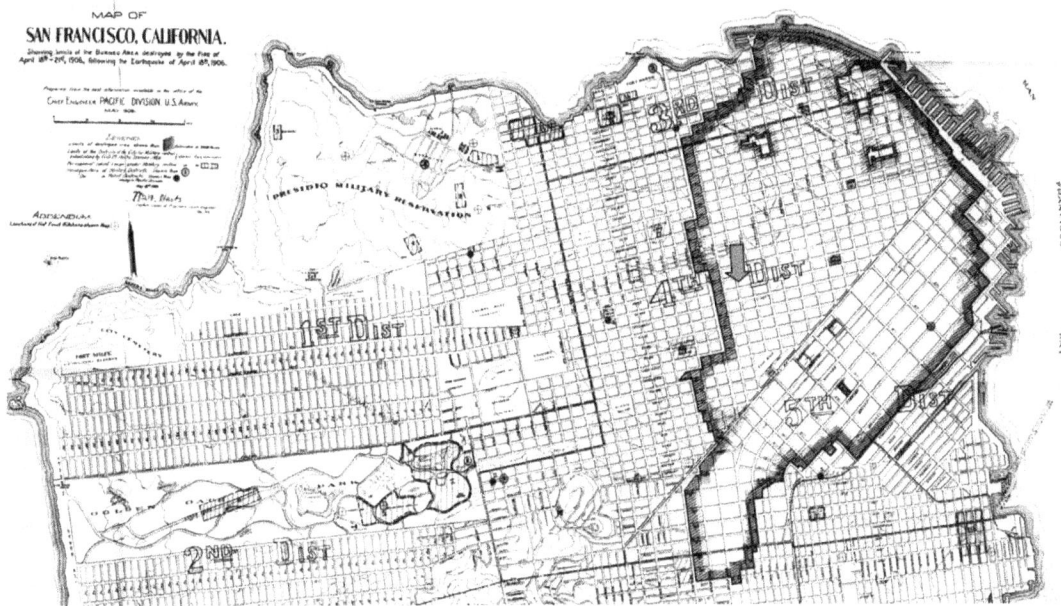

Historic map showing the area consumed by fire after the earthquake. The red arrow shows where the Afeld home and business was located. (U.S. Army, Pacific Division, May 1906.)

No records have provided clues as to where Elisabeth lived between the earthquake and 1913 where we find her in the San Francisco City Directory living at 230 Caselli Avenue. This address is about half a mile outside of the fire zone, off Market Street.

Around 1918 Elizabeth moved to Altenheim, a senior citizen resident community located in Oakland, California. While this would seem fairly commonplace, the census records show that the entire community was made up of immigrants from Germany, which would have been unique in the early 1900's. Elizabeth died in in 1929 and was likely buried at Green Lawn Cemetery in Colma, even though she is listed as being interred with Josef at San Francisco Columbarium.

About San Francisco Columbarium

The Columbarium was designed by architect Bernard J.S. Cahill and built in 1898. It was once part of the Odd Fellows Cemetery, which encompassed approximately 167 acres. In 1902 the San Francisco Board of Supervisors passed an ordinance that prohibited the sale of cemetery lots or allow any further burials within the city. The Odd Fellows established Green Lawn Cemetery in Colma and decided to move bodies in 1929. Many families also chose to remove their urns from the Columbarium. The crematorium and various mausoleums were demolished, and many of the headstones were used to build a seawall at Aquatic Park.

After a time, the Columbarium was sold to the Bay Cities Cemetery Association and later to Cypress Abbey. Over time, it fell into disrepair. In 1980, the Neptune Society of Northern California bought it and began restoration. In 1996, the building was added to the register of San Francisco Designated Landmarks.

Both Josef and Elisabeth have memorials at Find a Grave stating that they are at the Columbarium at Floor 2, Section I. Their memorial numbers are 62427985 and 62428039. A call to the Neptune Society yielded no information other than, "it is likely they were moved to the Colma site in 1929."

Chapter 4

The Afeld Brothers Come to America: Franz Wilhelm Afeld

Franz Wilhelm Afeld was baptized on September 10, 1826 at the Dom cathedral in Fulda, Germany.

Translation: Born and legitimately baptized, Franz Wilhelm Afeld, son of Adam Joseph Afeld, streetpaver, and Anna Maria Drinnenberg, who were married. Sponsor, Franz Michael Drinnenberg, brother.

He was born into a rapidly changing world at the end of the period known as the industrial revolution. In his homeland, Friedrich Wilhelm III was King of Prussia within the German Republic and ruled until his death in 1840.

Fulda is located about 55 miles northeast of Frankfurt, on the Fulda River. The town became prosperous when an abbey was founded there around 750 by Saint Boniface, whose crypt remains in the present day Dom cathedral. In 1752, the abbey was designated a bishopric, and its abbots became the prince-abbots and later, the prince-bishops. Under the guidance of the abbey, the town flourished, adding a university and a porcelain factory. The porcelain from this factory is sought after by collectors present day. In 1803, Napoleon disbanded all states under his territorial authority. After his defeat, several lower-level ruling families controlled the territory, including the Prince of Orange and the Duchy of Berg.

By 1825, the population grew to about 2,500. Fulda contained a palace and gardens, formerly the residence of the prince-bishops, a number of churches, two convents, an ecclesiastical seminary, and a number of schools. In his youth, it is easy to conclude that Franz attended school. We know that he could read, write, and knew enough arithmetic to run a successful business upon his arrival America.

When Franz left Germany for America in 1850, King Friedrich Wilhelm IV was on the throne, struggling with territorial wars and a population divided between maintaining a monarchy or creating a freely elected government.

View of Boniface Plaza and Main Station in Fulda in 1850. This is how Fulda would have appeared to Franz when he left for America. (Source: Original-Ansichten Kurfürstenthum Hessen, S. 592. Julius Lange (Zeichner); Johann Gabriel Friedrich Poppel (Stahlstecher).

No immigration record or passenger manifest has been located, but we have one clue as to the year, 1850, which is enumerated in the 1900 US Federal Census. Indeed, Franz is invisible in the records until 1863 where we find his Civil War draft registration and an entry in the New York City Directory. The directory entry reads, *Afield, Frances leafmaker, 12 Wooster*. The address is also that of his brother, Joseph. There is no evidence that Franz was called to service. Below is his Civil War draft registration entry.

Consolidated list of all persons of Class II, subject to do military duty in the Fourth Congressional District (8th ward), consisting of the county of New York and State of New York, enumerated during the month of June, 1863, under direction of Captain Joel B. Ernhardt, Provost Marshal.

According to church records, Adam Afeld, Franz's father, died in January 1851. It is unknown whether he returned to Germany for some period of time, although no passenger record was located that would confirm his re-entry into the United States.

Franz embraced the family business and we find that in 1868, city directory and tax records indicate that the business is called Afeld & Bro. and is located at 80 Greene Street in Manhattan.

Franz does not appear in the US Federal Census in 1860, 1870, or 1880, but there are addresses for him in multiple city directories.

1863	12 Wooster, New York
1871	109 Greene, New York
1873-74	12 Amity, New York
1874	32 Kendall Street, Boston
1875	9 Chapman Place, Boston
1877	197 Shawmut Avenue, Boston
1878	Removed to Philadelphia (in Boston City Directory)
1879	707 Wallace, Philadelphia
1900	59 West 11th Street, New York

In 1872, Franz married Theresa Sandbichler and a remarkable, two-page marriage record was generated. It provided the clues needed to research the Afeld family in Germany.

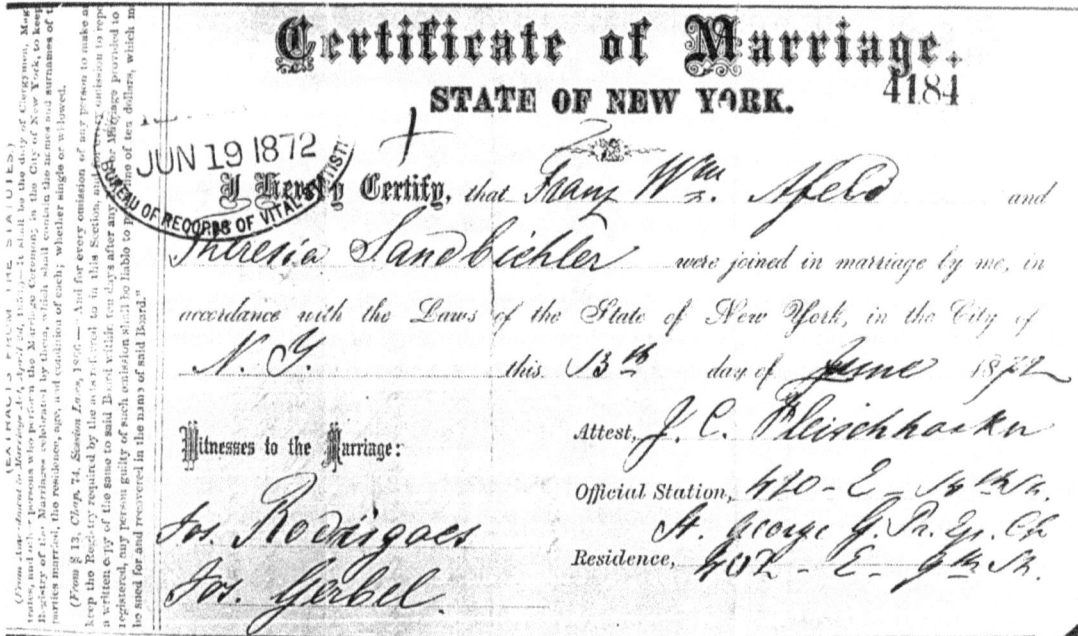

Certificate of Marriage.
STATE OF NEW YORK. 4184

JUN 19 1872

I Hereby Certify, that *Franz Wm. Afeld* and *Theresia Sandbichler* were joined in marriage by me, in accordance with the Laws of the State of New York, in the City of *N. Y.* this *13* day of *June* *1872*

Witnesses to the Marriage:

Jos. Rodrigues
Jos. Gerbel

Attest, *J. C. Fleischhacker*
Official Station, *420 - E. 14th St.*
St. George G. Pr. Ep. Ch.
Residence, *402 - E. 9th St.*

Witnesses to the Marriage: Joseph Rodrigues is the husband of Bertha Sandbichler, sister of Theresa. Joseph Gerbel is the husband of Adeline Sandbichler, sister of Theresa.

Minister: J. C. Fleishhacker; Official Station: 420 East 14th Street, St. George German Protestant Episcopal Church

The information below about Rev. Fleischhacker and St. George's Church, not only provides insight into the minister who married Franz and Theresa, but also lays bare the lengths to which immigrants transformed themselves in order to pursue freedom and opportunity in the United States. It is very likely that Franz and Theresa met at St. Geroge's or at one of their support programs.

About Rev. J. C. Fleischhacker

Rev. J. C. Fleischhacker was born in Germany in 1829 and died of pneumonia in New York City on February 15, 1886. He was educated for the ministry and spent several years in preaching in Germany, after which he went to Jerusalem, and was there with Bishop Gobat for nine years, devoting his time to missionary work. He came to the United States and became assistant to the Rev. Dr. Tyng in the German Mission Chapel between April 18, 1869 and May, 1878. For the next few years he held no regular position, but devoted his labors to missionary work among the people of his own nationality. (Anstice, Henry. 1911. History of St. George's Church in the city of New York, 1752-1811-1911, page 461. New York: Harper.)

About the German Ministry of St. George's Church

The Rev. Mr. Wolcott, who had labored so faithfully for eight years in the pioneer work, and had enjoyed the satisfaction of seeing ample provision made for its establishment on a permanent basis, was compelled by failing health to resign his charge, and the Rev. C. W. Bolton was appointed in March, 1859, as minister of St. George's Chapel and the Rev. Charles Schramm, D.D., as minister in charge of the German department. The chapel proper seated about 800 people, the English congregation worshiping in the morning and evening and the German congregation in the afternoon.

Both Sunday-schools met in the morning in their respective rooms, the one numbering 380 attendants and the other 140. There was also maintained a daily English school of 130 children. A reading-room for men and boys was open every evening. There was a lecture Tuesday evening for the English congregation and a Prayer meeting Thursday evening. The German congregation had a lecture every Friday evening, and a sewing-school for both the English and the German girls was efficiently at work.

Meanwhile the thriving German Mission under the Rev. Dr.Schramm had utterly outgrown the accommodation which could be spared for it in the Nineteenth Street chapel. The rector and the Mission Trustees therefore, in January, 1863, purchased a lot of land and the building thereon in East Fourteenth Street for $3,700, altering and adapting it for the use of the German Mission at an expenditure of $7,000, which was supplied by St. George's Sunday school and friends in the congregation. It was ready for occupancy October 11, 1863, and was consecrated by Bishop Potter on Christmas eve. Dr. Schramm's connection with the Chapel terminated in March, 1869, after a connection with St. George's Mission work of sixteen years since his first entrance upon it as a teacher. The Rev. J. C. Fleischhacker was his successor.

The German work, demanding more facilities for growth, and the Chapel of the Bread of Life clamoring for room to expand, it was finally decided, after examining other sites, to buy a lot adjoining and replace the existing German chapel on Fourteenth Street by a larger two-storied building for the accommodation of them both. This plan was carried out in 1872, at a cost of $40,000, and the two Missions jointly occupied the new, commodious, and convenient chapel building. During the process of *erection the German congregation was accommodated in a hall in the Plympton Building, at Eighth Street and Astor Place.*

From the date of the joint occupancy of the new chapel with the German Mission, the Chapel of the Bread of Life, under the efficient superintendence of Mr. W. H. Philips, grew rapidly. In April, 1873, it numbered 32 teachers and 413 scholars, holding two sessions each Sunday. Within five years it had 68 teachers and 1,000 members on its roll, divided into three departments, with an average attendance of 800. A Sunday Evening Service was regularly held.

The mission work undertaken by the church was a critical part of enabling German immigrants to become a part of New York society. Through education and encouragement of self-help, they provided the foundation for entry into the middle class. A brief listing of programs includes, The Sewing School, The Helping Hand, The Dorcas Society, The Sewing Circle, The Mother's Meeting for the women and girls, The Day School for Children, The Debating Society, The Young Men's Literary Association, The Reading Room for boys and men; the Christmas Festivals, Thanksgiving Treats, and Summer Excursions,—all these bore their part, together with the Bible readers, parish visitors, prayer meetings, and other religious gatherings for instruction and worship, in the uplift of the families and neighborhoods to which the Chapels ministered.

Reverend Fleischhacker organized his congregation into an independent church in April, 1878.(Anstice, Henry. 1911. History of St. George's Church in the city of New York, 1752-1811-1911, pages 271-272. New York: Harper.)

The second page of the marriage license provides an unusual amount of detail for the time period. Below are transcriptions of a few of the lines that are harder to read due to the use of old German script.

For Franz,
Line 6: Place of Birth is Fulda, Hesse-Nassau, Prussia
Line 7: Father's Name is A. Joseph Afeld
Line 8: Mother's Maiden Name: Anna Maria nee Drinnenberg

For Theresa,
Line 14: Place of Birth is Gmünd, Bavaria
Line 15: Father's Name is Benedic Sandbichler
Line 16: Mother's Maiden Name is Maria Staeger

RETURN OF A MARRIAGE.

1. Full Name of HUSBAND, *Franz Wm Afeld*
2. Place of Residence, *12 Amity St.*
3. Age next Birthday, *45* years,
4. *Wh.*
5. Occupation, *Flower Manufacturer*
6. Place of Birth, *Fulda - Hessen - Nassau Prup.*
7. Father's Name, *A Joseph Afeld*
8. Mother's Maiden Name, *Anna Maria née Trinks*
9. No. of Husband's Marriage, *first*
10. Full Name of WIFE, *Theresa Sandbichler*
    Maiden Name, if a Widow, _____
11. Place of Residence, *69 S. Washington Square*
12. Age next Birthday, *21* years,
13. *Wh.*
14. Place of Birth, *Gmünd - Bavaria*
15. Father's Name, *Benedix Sandbichler*
16. Mother's Maiden Name, *Maria Geiger*
17. No. of Wife's Marriage, *first*

N. B.—At Nos. 4 and 13 state if Colored; if other races, specify what. At Nos. 9 and 17 state whether 1st, 2d, 3d, &c., Marriage of each.

New York, *13th June* 1872

We, the Husband and Wife named in the above Certificate, hereby Certify that the information given is correct, to the best of our knowledge and belief.

_____ (Husband.)

_____ (Wife.)

Signed in presence of *Jose Rodriguez*

and *Jos Herbel*

Marriage record of Franz Wilhelm Afeld and Theresa Sandbichler.

Six days short of their one-year wedding anniversary, their first child, Eugene Louis Afeld, was born in New York on June 7, 1873. Shortly thereafter, the family moved to Boston to expand the artificial flower business. This was about a year after the Great Boston Fire that leveled 65 acres of buildings in the financial district, and there were new opportunities for those with the capital to build and invest. Three children were born to Franz and Theresa while they lived in Boston; Norman in the spring of 1874, Oscar Frances (aka Oscar Charles Richard) born on March 19, 1875, and their first daughter, Amelia, born on March 11, 1877. In late 1877 or early 1878, the family moved to Philadelphia, where Norma J. Afeld was born in July of 1878.

Around 1883, the family moved back to New York. This was around the time of Max Sand's death (Theresa's father), which could have been the reason for the move.

1898 brought the Spanish American War, in which his brother Joseph was enlisted. It also brought the happy occasion of the first marriage among his children, that of Amelia to Frederick Marshall. They provided three grandchildren before Franz's death in 1904.

DIED.

AFELD.—Franz Wilhelm Afeld, on Nov. 2, 1904, in his 78th year, beloved husband of Theresa Afeld.

Funeral from his late residence, 162 East End Av., Friday, Nov. 4, at 1:30 P. M. Interment at convenience of family.

Source: The New York Times; Nov 3, 1904, pg. 9.

Death Record of Franz Wilhelm Afeld. New York City Municipal Archives.

About Theresa Sandbichler

Theresa Sandbichler was born in Gmund, Germany on August 30, 1850. Her parents were Benedick Maximillian Sandbichler and Anna Maria Staeger. She arrived in New York on July 16, 1867 with her family. See chapter 5 for more information about her parents and siblings.

Sometime between 1905 and 1910, Theresa made the journey west to Los Angeles and lived with her daughter, Norma, and her family. She is enumerated there in the 1910 US Federal Census and appears in several Los Angeles City Directories through the year 1917. Her next appearance in a public record is not until the 1925 New York State Census where she and her son Charles reside at 572 Prospect Place in Brooklyn. This particular census asked about your citizenship status. An "A" is recorded for Thersa, meaning that she was not a nautralized citizen.

New York State Archives; Albany, New York; State Population Census Schedules, 1925; Election District: 53; Assembly. District: 11; City: Brooklyn; County: Kings; Page: 14.

She is recorded as a guest in the wedding announcement of her grandson, Walter Afeld, to Vivian Edna Ham in April 1926. Theresa died later that year on October 20th.

Theresa Sandbichler Afeld.

AFELD – Theresa, beloved mother of Amelia, Eugene and Charles, on Oct. 20, at the residence of her son, 572 Prospect Place, Brooklyn. Funeral at convenience of family. (New York Times, October 21, 1926, page 25.)

Franz and Theresa are buried at St. Michael's Cemetery (section 3, row 5, plot 11). Their son, Eugene, and his wife, Olga Antony, are buried next to them. They all share the same headstone.

About St. Michael's Cemetery

St. Michael's Cemetery is situated in the borough of Queens in New York City. Established in 1852, St. Michael's is one of the oldest religious, nonprofit cemeteries in the New York City metropolitan area which is open to people of all faiths. It is owned and operated by St. Michael's Church, an Episcopal congregation located on the Upper West Side of Manhattan.

The original property for St. Michael's Cemetery was purchased in 1852 by the Rev. Thomas McClure Peters and occupied seven acres. Over the years St. Michael's gradually acquired additional land to reach its present size of approximately eighty-eight acres.

About the Business, Afeld & Bro.

The actual opening date for the business was not determined, however, the first listing in New York City directories is in 1860. It is clear that Franz and Joseph worked together on the business and, for a time, shared living accommodations.

Afeld & Bro. appears in an 1866 excise tax assessment roll for the State of New York. The business was assessed $6.67.

The National Archives and Records Administration; Washington, D.C.; Internal Revenue Assessment Lists for New York and New Jersey, 1862-1866; Series: M603; Roll: 58; Description: District 4; Monthly and Special Lists; July-Dec 1866.

Beginning in 1871, the records show that Joseph is no longer with the artificial flower business. Instead, we find him in the New York City directories through 1875 at 355 Bowery, as the owner of a musical instrument store, an occupation that he keeps throughout a transcontinental move to San Francisco and his lifetime.

Beginning in 1871, the city directory indicates that Max Sand (aka Benedic Maximillian Sandbichler), Franz's father-in-law, is in the artificial flower business at the Afeld business address. Perhaps he came into the business when Joseph transitioned out. Max remains with the business through his death around 1884.

FRANZ AFELD,

MANUFACTURER OF

ARTIFICIAL FLOWERS, LEAVES,

NOVELTIES ETC.

20 WEST FOURTH STREET,
162 EAST END AVE.,
Cor. 87th St., NEW YORK

The business card of Franz Afeld, about 1900, showing two business locations.

In 1874, Franz moved the family to Boston and is engaged in the artificial flower business there. It's unclear if this is a separate venture or if he is merely selling the product being made in New York. He remains there until 1878, when he moves to Philadelphia and is engaged there for a number of years before returning to New York about 1883. From then until his death in 1904, he is listed in city directories with an occupation of artificial flowers. It is unclear if the business was closed or sold.

Chapter 5

The First Generation: Eugene Franz Louis Afeld

Eugene Afeld was born in Manhattan on June 7 or 8, 1873. There are several conflicting records for both his date of birth and his full name.

The first record is a birth record in Manhattan that provides the following information:

Name: Eugin Franz Afeld
Sex: Male
Birth: Date: June 8, 1873
Father: Franz W. Afeld
Mother: Theresa Sanbiegler

"New York, Births and Christenings, 1640-1962," index, FamilySearch , Eugin Franz Afeld, 08 Jun 1873; citing Manhattan, New York, New York, USA, reference ; FHL microfilm 1322064.

The second record is a birth registration in Boston, Massachusetts. It's unclear why his birth was registered a second time.

Certificate: 6519
Birth: June 7, 1873
Name: Eugene Afeld
Sex and Condition: Male
Place of Birth: New York City
Names of Parents: Franz Theresa
Residence of Parents: Boston
Occupation of Father: Artificial Flowers
Place of Birth of Father: Germany
Place of Birth of Mother: Germany

Ancestry.com. Massachusetts, Town and Vital Records, 1620-1988 [database on-line]. Provo, UT, USA. Original data: Town and City Clerks of Massachusetts.

There's no doubt that both records are for the same Eugene Afeld, given the uniqueness of names and his father's occupation. We know from the records that the family moved from Manhattan to Boston around 1873. The most likely scenario is that the record filed in Manhattan comes from the midwife who delivered Eugene and that the middle name "Franz" is what his parents provided at the time.

The second record in Boston was probably completed by Franz and Theresa when they realized that they had not registered his birth before they left New York. It, however, does not provide any middle name. In the 1900 US Census, he is enumerated with a middle initial "L" and then in 1918, his World War I Draft Registration provides the full middle name "Louis", which he used for the remainder of his life.

Eugene Louis Afeld in 1923. This photo was used for his Passport Application.

After the sudden death of his brother, Norman, Eugene married his widow, Olga C. Antony, who was already pregnant with Norman's son, Walter, who was born in 1901. No marriage record was found in Manhattan, Brooklyn, or Bronx for the years 1901 – 1903 at the New York City Municipal Archives.

About Olga C. Antony
Detailed information about Olga and her ancestors from Norway can be found in Chapter 7 – The Antony Family of Norway.

By the time the 1910 US Census was taken, Eugene and Olga already had what would be their full family. Along with Eugene and Olga is Walter, age 9, Robert, age 7, and Helen, age 3. Helen was born in New Jersey, so the family relocated sometime between 1904 and 1907. They reside at 35 Maple Street in Clifton, New Jersey. Eugene is employed as a clerk in a Drygoods store.

While Eugene was too old to serve, the US required registration for the World War I Draft in 1918. We do learn from this document that the family now resides at 209 Howe Avenue in Passaic, New Jersey and that his occupation is Assistant Manager at the Linen Thread Company in New York City.

World War I Selective Service System Draft Registration Cards, 1917-1918. Washington, D.C.: National Archives and Records Administration. M1509, 4,582 rolls. Registration State: New Jersey; Registration County: Passaic; Roll: 1754425; Draft Board: 2.

Eugene applied for a US Passport in May 1923 for the purpose of traveling to Great Britain on behalf of his employer. He declared that he had booked passage on the SS Cedric from New York on June 2, 1923. On the second page is a physical description of Eugene and an Affidavit of Birth is on page three, signed by his brother Oscar.

The rules should be carefully read before mailing the application to the Department of State, Division of Passport Control, Washington, D. C.

applicant all necessary information and guidance.

UNITED STATES OF AMERICA.

STATE OF _New York_
COUNTY OF _New York_ } ss.

A# *Afeld*

I, _Eugene Louis Afeld_, a NATIVE AND LOYAL CITIZEN OF THE UNITED STATES, hereby apply to the Department of State, at Washington, for a passport.

I solemnly swear that I was born at _New York_, in the State of _New York_, on or about the _7th_ day of _June_, 18_73_;* that my {father/husband} _Franz W. Afeld_, was born in _Germany_ and is now residing at _Deceased – 1904_

*that he emigrated to the United States from the port of _____ on or about _____, 1____; that he resided _____ years, uninterruptedly, in the United States, from 1____ to 1____, at _____; that he was naturalized as a citizen of the United States before the _____ Court of _____, at _____, on _____, 1____, as shown by the accompanying Certificate of Naturalization]; that I have resided outside of the United States at the following places for the following periods; _never outside_, from _____ to _____; from _____ to _____

and that I am domiciled in the United States, my permanent residence being at _Passaic_, 209 Howe Ave in the State of _New Jersey_, where I follow the occupation of _Department Manager_

My last passport was obtained from _none_, on _____ and was _____ I am about to go abroad temporarily; and I
(Disposition of passport.)
intend to return to the United States within _two_ {months/years} with the purpose of residing and performing the duties of citizenship therein; and I desire a passport for use in visiting the countries hereinafter named for the following purpose:

Great Britain _Commercial business for_
(Name of country.) (Object of visit.)
_____ _The Linen Thread Co._
(Name of country.) (Object of visit.)
_____ _96 Franklin St. New York City_
(Name of country.) (Object of visit.)

I intend to leave the United States from the port of _New York_
(Port of departure.)
sailing on board the _s/s Cedric_ on _June 2d_, 1923
(Date of departure.)

OATH OF ALLEGIANCE.

Further, I do solemnly swear that I will support and defend the Constitution of the United States against all enemies, foreign and domestic; that I will bear true faith and allegiance to the same; and that I take this obligation freely, without any mental reservation or purpose of evasion; So help me God.

Eugene Louis Afeld
(Signature of applicant.)

Sworn to before me this _____ day of _MAY 1 - 1923_, 192___

[SEAL OF COURT.]

Philip H. Ahrens

Agent (Clerk) of the Department of State. Court of

MAY 4- 1923

2347

DESCRIPTION OF APPLICANT.

Age: _4 9_ years.

Stature: _5_ feet, _9_ inches, Eng.

Forehead: _medium_

Eyes: _brown_

Nose: _medium_

Distinguishing marks _____

Mouth: _medium_

Chin: ~~medium~~ _round_

Hair: _black and gray_

Complexion: _fair_

Face: _oblong_

IDENTIFICATION.

May 1, 19_23_

I, _Leslie T. Jennings_ solemnly swear that I am a { native ~~naturalized~~ } citizen of the United States; that I reside at _Brooklyn N.Y._ : that I have known the above-named _Eugene L. Afeld_ personally for _5_ years and know { him ~~her~~ } to be a native citizen of the United States; and that the facts stated in { his ~~her~~ } affidavit are true to the best of my knowledge and belief.

No lawyer or other person will be accepted as witness to a passport application if he has received or expects to receive a fee for his services in connection with the execution of the application or obtaining the passport.

Leslie T. Jennings

Messenger
(Occupation.)

1106 Lorimer St. Brooklyn
(Address of witness.)

Sworn to before me this _____ day

of _MAY 1 - 1923_, 19___

[SEAL.]

Philip H. Ahrens

Agent of the Department of State

~~Clerk of the~~ _____ Court at _____

Applicant desires passport to be sent to the following address:

209 Howe Ave.

Passaic

New Jersey

AFFIDAVIT OF BIRTH TO BE SUBMITTED WITH APPLICATION
FOR AMERICAN PASSPORT

NOTE.—A very severe penalty is provided in Sections 2 and 4 of Title 9 of the Espionage Act approved June 2, 1917, for the falsification of applications for passports, or of affidavits or other documents to be used in connection therewith.

I, the undersigned, do solemnly swear that to the best of my knowledge and belief the following statements are true and correct:

That I have known _____ *Eugene L. Afeld* _____
(Name of person whose birth in the U. S. is to be proved.)

who ~~whose wife~~ } is an applicant for an American passport, for the past _____ *40* _____ years:

That the person whose name appears above is now

~~deceased.~~ residing at } _____ *209 Howe St Passaic N. J.* _____
(Street address and city or town.) (State.)

and was born in _____ *New York* _____ , _____ *N Y* _____
(City or town.) (State.)

on or about _____ *June 7* _____ , _____ *1873* _____ , and is my _____ *Brother* _____
(Month and date.) (Year.) (Name relationship or write "Not related.")

My knowledge and belief of place and date of birth appearing above are based upon the following facts:
(If affiant is not related to person whose birth in the U. S. is to be proved state briefly how and through what source the knowledge was acquired.)

_____ *Oscar C Afeld* _____
(Signature of affiant.)

_____ *Letter Carrier New York City* _____
(Occupation and name of firm.)

_____ *Wall St P.O.* _____
(Street address.)

_____ *New York, N. Y.* _____
(City and State.)

Subscribed and sworn to before me this _____ *2nd* _____ day of _____ *May* _____ , 192 *3*

_____
(Agent of the Department of State) or (Notary Public.)

IMPORTANT—Use impression seal.]

Name of Ship _____ "CELTIC" _____   Date of Departure _____ 192_

Steamship Line _____ WHITE STAR _____   Where Bound _____ NEW YORK

NAMES AND DESCRIPTIONS OF ALIEN PASSENGERS EMBARKED AT THE PORT OF LIVERPOOL

B.—NON-TRANSMIGRANTS, *that is Alien Passengers other than those included under* **A.**

Contract Ticket Number	NAMES OF PASSENGERS.	Last Address in the United Kingdom.	Adults	Children	Infants	CLASS (Whether 1st, 2nd, or 3rd.)	Port at which Passengers have contracted to land.	Profession, Occupation, or Calling of Passengers.	Ages of Passengers (Adults)	Ages (Children 1 and 12)	Ages (Infants)	Country of which Citizen or Subject.	Country of Last Permanent Residence.	Country of Intended Future Permanent Residence.
192281	Mstr Francisco Pardo	c/o White Star Line, Liverpool	1			1st	New York	Child		8		Spain	1	U.S.A.
" 2	Mr Ricardo Capico	"	1			"	"	s.s. Agent	39			U.S.A.	1	"
"	Mrs Aquilina C	"	1			"	"	Wife	41			"	1	"
"	Miss Aquilina "	"		1		"	"	Child		9		"	1	"
"	Mstr Manuel "	"		1		"	"	"		8		"	1	"
"	Miss Teresa "	"		1		"	"	"		6		"	1	"
"	Estefania "	"		1		"	"	"		5		"	1	"
"	Mstr Jose "	"		1		"	"	"		10		"	1	"
194916	Mr Albert Addie	Savoy Hotel, London	1			"	"	Lawyer	59			"	1	"
"	Mrs Katherine "	"	1			"	"	Wife Asst	40			"	1	"
59305	Miss May Sibley	c/o Am. Express Co, London	1			"	"	Librarian	47			"	1	"
197104	Mr Ignatius Alexander Schneider	57, Bishopsgate, London	1			"	"	Secy	48			C.Slovakia	1	England
197118	Eugene Afeld	Victoria Hotel, London W.C.	1			"	"	Merchant	50			U.S.A.	1	U.S.A.

Eugene stayed at the Victoria Hotel in Westminster while in London. He departed from Liverpool, England, on June 30, 1923 aboard the SS Celtic, a ship in the White Star Line, in first class. He arrived at the Port of New York on July 8th.

Eugene and Olga remained in the same house at 209 Howe Avenue for the next 20 years. In 1930, they declared a home value of $4,000 and their daughter, Helen, still resides with them and is employed as a "telephone operator". Eugene has gone back to work as a salesman for the Drygoods store.

Olga Antony Afeld and Eugene Afeld with their grandchildren, Robert and Hollis, in 1935.

Olga died on August 17, 1946 and Eugene died in Gulfport, Florida on February 8, 1947 at age 73. He was interred in a family plot at St. Michael's Cemetery in with wife, Olga, and his parents, Franz and Theresa (Sandbichler) Afeld.

Saint Michael's Cemetery, East Elmhurst, Queens County, New York. Section 3, Row 5, Grave 11.

Descendants of Eugene Franz Louis Afeld and Olga C. Antony

Eugene Franz Louis Afeld and Olga C. Antony had the following children:

1) Robert John Afeld
2) Helen M. Afeld

Generation 2

1) Robert John Afeld was born on September 3, 1903 in Bronx, New York. He died in 1948 in Gulfport, Pinellas, Florida. He married Rose Cecilia Morris, who was born in 1903 in New York City. She was the daughter of Michael Morris and Rose Casey, both of whom were born in Ireland. She died in March 1960 in Pinellas County, Florida.

Marriage Record of Robert Afeld and Rose C. Morris. New York City Municipal Archives.

Robert and Rose lived in Bronx, New York in 1930 at 3536 Hall Avenue with their first child, Robert. He is employed as a clerk at a Brokerage house. The family relocated to 14 Summit Road in Clifton, Passaic, New Jersey sometime before

1932. He is employed as a "stock trader" in 1940 and reported that he worked the entire year in 1939. The family appears to have fared well during the Depression given his profession in the stock market.

Fifteenth Census of the United States, 1930. Washington, D.C.: National Archives and Records Administration, 1930. T626, 2,667 rolls. Year: 1930; Census Place: Bronx, Bronx, New York; Roll: 1489; Page: 2B; Enumeration District: 0675; Image: 380.0; FHL microfilm: 2341224.

Sixteenth Census of the United States, 1940. Washington, D.C.: National Archives and Records Administration, 1940. T627, 4,643 rolls. Year: 1940; Census Place: Clifton, Passaic, New Jersey; Roll: T627_2375; Page: 13A; Enumeration District: 16-9A.

Robert John Afeld and Rose Cecilia had the following children:

> **3)** Robert E. Afeld
> **4)** Richard Afeld
> **5)** Raymond Walter Afeld

2) Helen M. Afeld was born in 1907 in Plainfield, Union, New Jersey. She died about 1961 in New Jersey. She married Winthrop Chase Wood on January 24, 1931 in Manhattan, New York. He was born on February 9, 1896 in Fall River, Bristol, Massachusetts and he died on March 27, 1977 in Bloomfield, Essex, New Jersey.

Winthrop Chase Wood and Helen M. Afeld had the following child:

> **6)** Joan Wood was born on August 15, 1932 in Bloomfield, Essex, New Jersey. She died on January 10, 2009 in Bloomfield, Essex, New Jersey.

Generation 3

3) Robert E. Afeld was born on June 2, 1928 in New York. He died on January 2, 1985 in Clearwater, Florida at age 56. He married Harriet Anne Gause on November 26, 1950 in St. Petersburg, Florida.

Harriet Anne Gause was born on July 9, 1929 and she died on April 11, 2006 in Raleigh, North Carolina. She was buried in Clearwater, Florida at Calvary Catholic Cemetery and Mausoleum.

AFELD, ROBERT E., 56, of 1591 Scott St., Clearwater, formerly of Gulfport, died Wednesday (Jan. 2, 1985). Born in New York City, he came to Pinellas County in 1945 from New Jersey and was a former Winn-Dixie store manager. He was a member of Light of Christ Catholic Church, Democratic Executive Committee and Northern Pinellas Democratic Club, all of Clearwater. Survivors include his wife Harriet Anne; three daughters, Carolyn Anita Lacey, Littleton, Colo., Cynthia A. Afeld, Butler, Pa., and Donna M. Frazho, Dunedin; a brother Raymond W., St.

Petersburg, and two grandchildren. R. Lee Williams Funeral Home, St. Petersburg. (St. Petersburg Times, Friday, January 4, 1985, volume 101, number 164, page 15B.)

Robert Afeld and Harriet Anne Gause had the following children:

   7) Carolyn Anita Afeld
   8) Donna M. Afeld
   9) Cinthia A. Afeld

4) Richard Afeld was born on July 23, 1933 in New Jersey. He died on December 18, 1982 in Pinellas County, Florida at age 49. He married (1) Charlotte R. Dachtler, who was born on January 14, 1934 in Wiesbaden, Biebrich Hessen, West Germany.

AFELD, RICHARD "DICK", 49, of 4808 28th Ave. S., Gulfport, died Saturday (Dec. 18, 1982). Born in Passaic, N.J., he came here in 1947 from Clifton, N.J. and was comptroller of Summit Systems of Tampa College and retired as a master sergeant from the U.S. Air Force, after 24 years' service. He was third vice president and former secretary of Gulfport Lions Club, and a member of Holy Name Catholic Church, Gulfport. Survivors include his wife Charlotte; a son James E., Clearwater, and Raymond W., St. Petersburg. H. Glenn Hendley Funeral Home, Gulfport. (St. Petersburg Times, Sunday, December 29, 1982, volume 99, number 148, page 25B.)

Richard Afeld and Charlotte R. Dachtler had the following child:

   10) James R. Afeld

5) Raymond Walter Afeld was born on December 17, 1935 in New Jersey. He married Doris Emily Doubek, daughter of James and Mary Doubek, in July 1956 in Pinellas County, Florida. She was born on June 17, 1938 in Florida.

Raymond Walter Afeld and Doris Emily Doubek had the following children:

   11) Deborah Jean Afeld
   12) Daniel James Afeld
   13) Patricia Rosemary Afeld
   14) Robert Shawn Afeld

Generation 4

The family of Raymond and Doris. Row 1: Danny, Doris, Cade, Raymond, Debbie. Row 2: Taylor, Erica, Sean, Richard. Row 3: Cindy, Zachary, Patty, Emily, Richard, Kaylee.

11) Deborah Jean Afeld was born on December 18, 1957. She married Richard Arthur Mace on June 5, 1976 in Pinellas County, Florida.

Deborah Afeld and Richard Mace had he following children:

15) Richard Arthur Mace, Jr.
16) Kendra Leigh Mace

12) Daniel James Afeld was born on February 13, 1959. He married Cynthia Lee Newberne on December 3, 1983 in Pinellas County, Florida.

Daniel James Afeld and Cynthia Lee Newberne had the following children:

17) Jaclyn Rebecca Afeld
18) Jaimee Lee Afeld

13) Patricia Rosemary Afeld was born on September 21, 1962. She married Walter Allan Poole on June 6, 1987 in Pinellas County, Florida.

Walter Allan Poole and Patricia Rosemary Afeld had the following children:

19) Kaylee Nicole Poole
20) Emily Lauren Poole

14) Robert Shawn Afeld was born on May 26, 1966. He married (1) Angela Musette Russo on July 22, 1995 in Hillsborough County, Florida. He married (2) Erica Dawn Daugherty on September 26, 1999 in Hillsborough County, Florida.

Robert Shawn Afeld had the following children:

21) Zachary Jacob Hodges
22) Taylor Nicole Hodges
23) Cade Robert Afeld

Chapter 6

The First Generation: Norman Afeld

Norman was likely born Between March and May of 1874, and most likely in Boston, Massachusetts. The date is surmised from the dates of birth for his siblings, Eugene and Oscar, and the fact that the family moved to Boston for business at that time. It is remotely possible that he was born in New York, since his father's business operations were still headquartered there, but no birth certificate has been located in either jurisdiction. Archivists at the Municipal Archives in New York City searched between 1872 (the year of marriage of his parents) and 1877 (the year his sister Amelia is born in Boston and for which we have documentation). The Birth Registers in Boston also did not contain an entry for him.

He is not enumerated in the 1900 US Census with his parents, so it is likely that he had moved out and was living on his own in New York City or across the river in New Jersey, although no entries were identified in the City Directory's in New York or New Jersey. It was about this time that he met Olga Antony, who lived with her family in the Jersey City area.

Their son, Walter Eugene Afeld, was born on December 2, 1901, in New York City. The birth certificate gives a residential address for each parent and both are recorded as 967 Washington Avenue, New York. It also records his occupation as "clerk" but gives no business name or industry.

No marriage record for Norman and Olga has been located. Archivists searched the period between 1899 and 1901. According to Afeld family stories, Norman died shortly before Walter's birth. It is therefore possible that the couple were never officially married. No death record, obituary, or burial record has been located. Again, archivists in New York searched the time period 1900 to 1902. The death and obituary listings in The New York Times were also searched.

All-in-all, we know almost nothing about Norman. Other than the birth certificate of his son, no other record bearing his name has been located.

Second Generation

Walter Eugene Afeld

Norman and Olga Afeld welcomed their first child, Walter Eugene Afeld, into the world on December 2, 1901. Walter was born at his parents' home at 967 Washington Avenue in the Borough of the Bronx, New York.

Name.	Walter Eugene Afeld
Sex.	Male
Color.	White
Date of Birth.	Dec 2 1901
Place of Birth.	967 Wash Ave
Father's Name.	Norman Afeld
Residence.	967 Wash Ave
Birthplace.	U. S.
Age.	27
Occupation.	Clerk
Mother's Name.	Olga Afeld
Mother's Name before Marriage.	" Antony
Residence.	967 Wash
Birthplace.	Norway
Age.	28
Number of previous Children.	0
How many now living (in all).	1
Date of Record.	Dec 16 1901

Source: New York City Department of Records, Municipal Archives, New York, New York. Certificate number 3899.

His father, Norman, died either within a few months of his birth and possibly even a few months prior. Olga relocated the family to Passaic, New Jersey, where we find them enumerated in the 1910 US Federal Census. Olga's mother and step-father lived nearby.

In April 1926, Walter married Vivian Edna Ham, the only child of Perley D. Ham and Emma B. Littlefield. According to a wedding announcement in a local newspaper, the ceremony was performed at the bride's home, 48 Maple Place, in Clifton, by Rev. Francis Gerritsen, pastor of the First Presbyterian Church of Garfield, in the presence of eighty relatives and friends.

The announcement of their marriage, drafted by the mother of the bride, appeared in local papers in April 1926. It is included here in its entirety because of the significant number of family, friends, and business associates included.

Miss Vivian Edna Ham Is Bride Of W. E. Afeld At Home Ceremony

Rev. Mr. Gerritsen, of Garfield Presbyterian Church, Officiates – Bride's Gown Beautiful – Miss Afeld Maid of Honor; Robert Afeld Best Man – To Reside In Maple Place, Clifton.

Miss Vivian Edna Ham, only daughter of Mr. and Mrs. Perley D. Ham, of 18 Maple Place, Clifton, on Saturday evening became the bride of Walter Eugene Afeld, son of Mr. and Mrs. Eugene L. Afeld, of 209 Howe Avenue, Passaic. The ceremony was performed at the bride's home at 8'oclock by the Rev. Francis Gerritsen, pastor of the First Presbyterian Church of Garfield, in the presence of eighty relatives and friends.

The "Bridal Chorus" from Lohengrin was played by Mrs. Charles Horn of Clifton, as the bride entered the living room on the arm of her father, who gave her in marriage. She was charming in a gown of Chantilly lace over white satin, the lace of the skirt falling in ripples. A spray of white satin flowers decorated the right shoulder.

The coronet veil of bridal lace was made in Dutch cap effect, shirred softly on the head with maline, and caught that each side of the neck and at the wrists with orange blossoms. The bridal bouquet was white sweet peas with a center of yellow roses.

The bride's only attendant was Miss Helen Afeld, of Passaic, sister of the groom, as maid of honor. Miss Afeld wore a gown of maize colored Romaine crepe, beaded. Her slippers and hose were of silver. Her hair ornament was a wreath of rhinestone leaves and she carried Ophelia roses. Robert Afeld attended his brother as best man.

The ceremony was performed before the living room fireplace. Tall palms were on either side and an artistic banking of Easter lilies, ferns, and yellow spring flowers, made a beautiful setting. The entire house was lovely with green foliage, yellow daffodils, and pussy willows effectively placed by Sceery, of Passaic. Charles Horn, of Clifton, sang D'Hardelot's "Because" before the ceremony. Mendelssohn's Wedding March was played after the ceremony.

A reception followed, with Mr. and Mrs. Ham and Mr. and Mrs. Afeld in the receiving line with the bridal party. A buffet supper was served by Caterer Walker, of Patterson. Later Mr. and Mrs. Afeld left for a wedding trip of two week's duration, during which they will visit Atlantic City, Washington and points in Virginia. On the return the young couple will reside at 48 Maple Place, Clifton.

Mrs. Afeld is a graduate of the Hasbrouck Heights High School, she is still a popular member of the younger social set in Garfield where the family resided for many years, and has made warm friends during her Clifton residence. Mr. Afeld is a salesman for the J. L. Prescott Company, of which firm Mr. Ham is superintendent.

The invited guests were: Mr. and Mrs. E. Matthers, Mr. and Mrs. W. C. Snyder, Mr. and Mrs. Austin Cowles, Mr. and Mrs. Arthur Mueller, Miss Florence Sisco, Mrs. Etta Troast, Mr. and Mrs. Charles Horn, Stanley Lucas, Miss Edna Buckhout, and Mr. and Mrs. Edgar Burbank, all of Clifton.

The Rev. Francis Gerritsen and Mrs. Gerritsen, Mr. and Mrs. George H. Wright, Mr. and Mrs. Charles W. Forss, and Mr. and Mrs. William Forss, all of Garfield; Mr. and Mrs. Harold Hutchinson, of Hawthorne; Mr. and Mrs. Julius Kramer, of Buenos Aires, S. A.; Charles Knowel, Miss Rose Morris, Charles Afeld, Mrs. H. Behn, Mrs. Teresa Afeld, E. A. Meyer, Miss Anna Borklund, the goal of New York City; Frank W. Lehman, Jr., of Woodridge; Mr. and Mrs. Fred Sanborn, of Mansfield, Mass.; Theodore Erickson, of Watertown, Mass.; Virgil Tobey, Junior Tobey, Mr. and Mrs. Eugene Tobey, Mr. and Mrs. Elmer Tobey, and Mr. and Mrs. Ralph Farnsworth, all of Everett, Mass.

Mr. and Mrs. Harry Goodrich, of Palmyra, Maine; Mr. and Mrs. Calvin Cole, of Dover, N. H.; Mr. and Mrs. Earl Coburn, of Elmhurst, L. I., Mr. and Mrs. O. F. Hayford, of Biddleford, Maine; Mr. and Mrs. Chester Furbish and Mr. and

Mrs. L. M. Ham, of North Berwick, Maine; Dr. L. V. Du Busc, of Elizabeth, N. J.; Mr. and Mrs. C. M. Lindsay. Of Montclair; Mr. and Mrs. Henry C. Fitch of East Rochester, N. H.; Mr. and Mrs. E. L. Afeld, Miss Helen Afeld, Robert Afeld, Mrs. O. Gerlach, Mr. and Mrs. Mortimer Weber.

Robert Prescott, Miss Olive Prescott, Mrs. J. E. Prescott, Mr. and Mrs. James L. Prescott, Mrs. Josephine Paisley, Mr. and Mrs. Ernest Goodrich, Mr. and Mrs. Harry Crawbuck, Mr. and Mrs. Matthew Geene, Miss Cornelia Greene, Miss Alma Greene, Mr. and Mrs. James Groendyk and Mr. and Mrs. Peter Greene, all of Passaic; Mr. and Mrs. John Keyes, of Passaic Park.

Mr. and Mrs. Percy Smith, of Allwood; Arthur McCabe, of Newark; Miss Virginia Barnes, and William Hall, of Hasbrouck Heights; Miss Eliza Gova, of Princeton; and William Connor, of Red Bank.

About Vivian Edna Ham

Vivian was, at least, a fifth-generation Maine native, and was born on December 20, 1902 in Waterville, Maine. Her father, Perley, worked at a company that made shoe polish in Maine, before moving his family to Garfield, New Jersey. It is possible that the company expanded operations into New Jersey, as he followed the same occupation there at the J.L. Prescott Company, where he is superintendent in 1940.

Vivian eventually retired to Florida, residing in Gulfport. She died on December 13, 2000 at Saint Petersburg. She was cremated and her ashes were caste by her son, Hollis, in Pinellas County, Florida in 2001.

> ***AFIELD, VIVIAN E.,*** *97, of Gulfport died Wednesday (Dec. 13, 2000) at Egret Cove Center, St. Petersburg. Born in Waterville, Maine, she came here in 1950 from Clifton, N. J. She was a homemaker and was Protestant. Survivors include a son, Hollis W., and a granddaughter, Barbara Afield, both of St. Petersburg. National Cremation Society, St. Petersburg.*
>
> *St. Petersburg Times, December 14, 2000; Vol. 117, No. 143, p. 7B.*

While extensive research on the Ham line was not conducted, a four-generation pedigree chart for Vivian is on the next page.

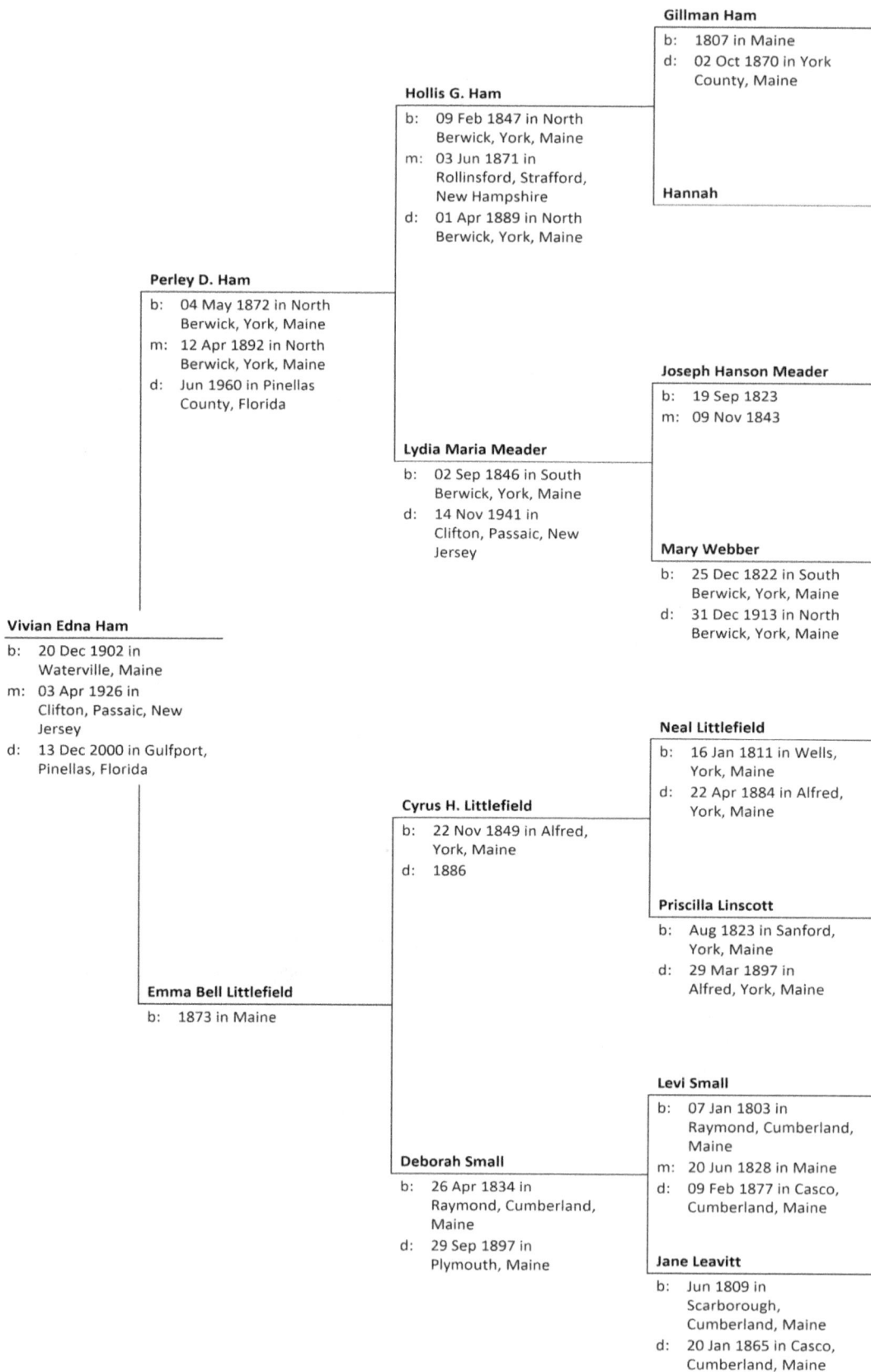

Gillman Ham

b: 1807 in Maine
d: 02 Oct 1870 in York County, Maine

Hollis G. Ham

b: 09 Feb 1847 in North Berwick, York, Maine
m: 03 Jun 1871 in Rollinsford, Strafford, New Hampshire
d: 01 Apr 1889 in North Berwick, York, Maine

Hannah

Perley D. Ham

b: 04 May 1872 in North Berwick, York, Maine
m: 12 Apr 1892 in North Berwick, York, Maine
d: Jun 1960 in Pinellas County, Florida

Joseph Hanson Meader

b: 19 Sep 1823
m: 09 Nov 1843

Lydia Maria Meader

b: 02 Sep 1846 in South Berwick, York, Maine
d: 14 Nov 1941 in Clifton, Passaic, New Jersey

Mary Webber

b: 25 Dec 1822 in South Berwick, York, Maine
d: 31 Dec 1913 in North Berwick, York, Maine

Vivian Edna Ham

b: 20 Dec 1902 in Waterville, Maine
m: 03 Apr 1926 in Clifton, Passaic, New Jersey
d: 13 Dec 2000 in Gulfport, Pinellas, Florida

Neal Littlefield

b: 16 Jan 1811 in Wells, York, Maine
d: 22 Apr 1884 in Alfred, York, Maine

Cyrus H. Littlefield

b: 22 Nov 1849 in Alfred, York, Maine
d: 1886

Priscilla Linscott

b: Aug 1823 in Sanford, York, Maine
d: 29 Mar 1897 in Alfred, York, Maine

Emma Bell Littlefield

b: 1873 in Maine

Levi Small

b: 07 Jan 1803 in Raymond, Cumberland, Maine
m: 20 Jun 1828 in Maine
d: 09 Feb 1877 in Casco, Cumberland, Maine

Deborah Small

b: 26 Apr 1834 in Raymond, Cumberland, Maine
d: 29 Sep 1897 in Plymouth, Maine

Jane Leavitt

b: Jun 1809 in Scarborough, Cumberland, Maine
d: 20 Jan 1865 in Casco, Cumberland, Maine

Walter and Vivian Edna Ham in 1929.

Their son, Hollis, was born on January 16, 1929. On April 8, 1930, Walter is enumerated in the US Census at his father-in-law's address. His occupation is listed as Manager of an Art Department in the silk industry.

Emma Littlefield Ham and Perley D. Ham (parents of Vivian Edna Ham) with their grandson, Hollis, in 1946.

Sometime in 1929, Walter met Molly McGovern, a successful vaudeville performer in New York. After dating some months, she married Walter in 1930 in Elkton, Maryland, where there was no waiting period between applying for a license and getting married. She later discovered that Walter, who had told her he was divorced, was not. Their son, Walter, was born in 1935.

About Evelyn "Molly" McGovern

Molly was born October 7, 1904 at Ballymote, County Sligo, Ireland to James McGovern and Margaret Egan. As a young woman, she immigrated to the US aboard the SS California.

The SS California entering harbor at New York in 1925.

The SS California was a British steamship that was built in Glasgow in 1923 for Henderson Brothers, a passenger steamship company. For most of her sea-going life, the California carried passengers between Glasgow and New York City. In 1935 she was sold to a subsidiary of the famous Cunard Lines, the Anchor Line. In As World War II loomed, she was requisitioned by the Admiralty and converted to an Armed Merchant Cruiser in 1939. She ferried troops through July 1943 when she was bombed by the German Luftwaffe and sunk in the North Atlantic.

LIST OR MANIFEST OF ALIEN PASSENGERS FOR THE UNITED

ALL ALIENS arriving at a port of continental United States (from a foreign port or a port of the insular possessions of the United States, and all aliens arriving at a port of said insular possessions from a foreign port, a port of continental United
This (white) sheet is for the listing of

S.S. "CALIFORNIA" . Passengers sailing from GLASGOW. , 18th. SEPTEMBER. , 192.

No. on List	HEAD-TAX STATUS	NAME IN FULL		Age		Married or single	Calling or occupation	Able to			Nationality	Race or people	Place of birth		Immigration Visa Number	Issued at	Date	Last permanent residence	
		Family name	Given name	Yrs.	Mos.	Sex							Country	City or town				Country	City or town
1		MacKay	George	61		M	S	Weigher	Yes	English	Yes	Britain	Scottish	Scotland	Carfin	20542	Glasgow	18/9/26	Scotland	Wishaw
2		McGregor	Martha	37		F	M	Housewife	Yes	English	Yes	Britain	Scottish	Scotland	Rutherglen	19904	Glasgow	20/8/26	Scotland	Dalmuir
3	UNDER 16	McGregor	Nelle	11		F	S	Nil	Yes	English	Yes	Britain	Scottish	Scotland	Dalmuir	19905	Glasgow	20/8/26	Scotland	Dalmuir
4	UNDER 16 or		Thomas	7		M	S	Nil	yes	English	Yes	Britain	Scottish	Scotland	Dalmuir	19906	Glasgow	20/8/26	Scotland	Dalmuir
5																				
6		Logan	Henry	21		M	S	Mechanic	Yes	English	Yes	Britain	Scottish	Scotland	Glasgow	19790	Glasgow	18/8/26	Scotland	Glasgow
7		Speirs	Agnes	21		F	M	Housewife	Yes	English	Yes	Britain	Scottish	Scotland	Renton	19546	Glasgow	10/8/26	Scotland	Clydebank
8	UNDER 16	Speirs	Thomas	6		M	S	School	Yes	English	Yes	Britain	Scottish	Scotland	Clydebank	19547	Glasgow	10/8/26	Scotland	Clydebank
9		Shaw	Jessie	27		F	M	Housewife Saleswoman	Yes	English	Yes	Britain	Scottish	Scotland	Glasgow	21887	Glasgow	8/9/26	Scotland	Glasgow
10		Sherry	Elizabeth	20		F	S		Yes	English	Yes	Britain	Scottish	Scotland	Glasgow	20250	Glasgow	2/9/26	Scotland	Glasgow
11		Williamson	James	26		M	S	Painter	Yes	English	Yes	Britain	Scottish	Scotland	Aberdeen	13244	Glasgow	6/8/26	Scotland	Burntisland
12		Hamilton	James	48		M	M	Stone Mason	Yes	English	Yes	Britain	Scottish	Scotland	Glasgow	20803	Glasgow	1/9/26	Scotland	Glasgow
13		Hamilton	Elizabeth	46		F	M	Housewife	Yes	English	Yes	Britain	Scottish	Scotland	Glasgow	20802	Glasgow	1/9/26	Scotland	Glasgow
14		Hamilton	Catherine	21		F	S	Weaver	Yes	English	Yes	Britain	Scottish	Scotland	Glasgow	20801	Glasgow	1/9/26	Scotland	Glasgow
15		Hamilton	Elizabeth	19		F	S	Domestic	Yes	English	Yes	Britain	Scottish	Scotland	Glasgow	20819	Glasgow	1/9/26	Scotland	Glasgow
16		Hamilton	Teresa	17		F	S	Weaver	Yes	English	Yes	Britain	Scottish	Scotland	Glasgow	20800	Glasgow	1/9/26	Scotland	Glasgow
17	UNDER 16	Hamilton	Agnes	15		F	S	Weaver	Yes	English	Yes	Britain	Scottish	Scotland	Glasgow	20804	Glasgow	1/9/26	Scotland	Glasgow
18	UNDER 16	Hamilton	John	14		M	S	School	Yes	English	Yes	Britain	Scottish	Scotland	Glasgow	20805	Glasgow	1/9/26	Scotland	Glasgow
19	UNDER 16	Hamilton	Mary	9		F	S	Nil	Yes	English	Yes	Britain	Scottish	Scotland	Glasgow	20806	Glasgow	1/9/26	Scotland	Glasgow
20	UNDER 16	Hamilton	Patricia	7		F	S	Nil	Yes	English	Yes	Britain	Scottish	Scotland	Glasgow	20807	Glasgow	1/9/26	Scotland	Glasgow
21		Maxwell	William	21		M	S	Moulder	Yes	English	Yes	Britain	Scottish	Scotland	Glasgow	20892	Glasgow	9/9/26	Scotland	Johnstone
22		Maxwell	Walter	19		M	S	Engineer	Yes	English	Yes	Britain	Scottish	Scotland	Glasgow	20892	Glasgow	9/9/26	Scotland	Johnstone
23																				
24		Robertson	John	21		M	S	Butcher	Yes	English	Yes	Britain	Scottish	Scotland	Inverness	11819	Glasgow	7/9/26	Scotland	Inverness
25		McKeown	Alexander	32		M	S	Miner Warehouse-	Yes	English	Yes	Britain	Scottish	Scotland	Edinburgh	12867	Glasgow	9/9/26	Scotland	Portobello
26		Park	John	18		M	S	man	Yes	English	Yes	Britain	Scottish	Scotland	Glasgow	20484	Glasgow	12/9/26	Scotland	Glasgow
27		Baglin	George	27		M	M	Miner	Yes	English	Yes	Britain	Scottish	Scotland	Motherwell	19195	Glasgow	27/7/26	Scotland	Blantyre
28		Crystal	Alexander	31		M	M	Miner	Yes	English	Yes	Britain	Scottish	Scotland	West Wemyss	13564	Glasgow	9/9/26	Scotland	West Wemyss
29		Mitchell	James	26		M	M	Baker	Yes	English	Yes	Britain	Scottish	Scotland	Greenock	20157	Glasgow	1/7/26	Scotland	Gourock
30		McGovern	Evelyn	22		F	S	Artist	Yes	English	Yes	Britain	Ireland	Ireland	Sligo	26145	Glasgow	8/8/26	Scotland	Glasgow

Line 5, Clemons Neulane, transferred to sheet 22 line 17
Line 22, John Robertson, transferred to sheet 8 line 29

FURBER

The S.S. California departed Glascow, Scotland, on September 18, 1926 and arrived at New York on September 27, 1926. Molly's entry in the passenger manifest is on line 30 (the last line), and contains the following information: Evelyn McGovern, age 22, female, single, Artist, able to read and speak English, white, resident of Britain, nationality is Irish, place of birth, Sligo, Ireland, travel visa number 26145, last permanent residence in Glascow, Scotland. We know that her address in Glascow was 16 Hutton Drive, as was recorded on her mother's passenger manifest entry under "Next of Kin."

She did not become a naturalized citizen until June 28, 1973, where a record appears in the Miami, Florida, courts. She died at age 81 in Tampa, Florida. She is buried at Sylvan Abbey in Clearwater, Florida.

Extensive research has been completed on the McGovern family history. See *Ballymote to Chicago* by John and Sylvia McCarrick.

In 1940, Walter, Vivian and Hollis are still living with her parents and it indicates that they have lived at the same residence since 1935. He is now a salesman for a chemical company where he worked the full year in 1939, earning a salary of $3,000, which converts to about $52,000 in 2014.

Walter Eugene Afeld in 1935.

Sometime between the 1940 US Census and a City Directory entry in 1951, Walter changed the spelling of the family name from Afeld to Afield. In June 1949, Walter took Vivian and their son, Hollis, to her parent's house in Florida and, according to divorce records, never returned.

Below are sections of the divorce proceedings filed by Vivian Edna Ham Afeld. The full transcript may be obtained from the Clerk of Courts, Hillsborough County, Forida.

IN THE CIRCUIT COURT OF HILLSBOROUGH COUNTY FLORIDA.

DIVISION G. No. 86576

VIVIAN EDNA AFELD,

Plaintiff

vs.

Divorce

Filed & Docketed

WALTER EUGENE AFELD

AUG 25 1950

Defendant.

~~CHAS H. PENT~~, Clerk

~~D. C.~~

Bill of Complaint.

Comes now, Vivian Edna Afeld, a resident of the State of Florida, by her attorney, Billie B. Bush, and brings this her complaint against the defendant, Walter Eugene Afeld, a non resident of the State of Florida and who resides at Passaic New Jersey, and complaining says:

1.

That plaintiff is and has been a bona fide resident of the State of Florida continuously for more than ninety days immediately preceding, the filing of this suit for divorce.

2.

That plaintiff and the defendant were lawfully married April 3rd, 1926, and ever since have been and now are husband and wife.

3.

That no child or children have been born the issue of said marriage except a son, Hollis Walter Afeld who is more than 21 years of age and is not legally dependent upon plaintiff or the defendant for his support.

79

4.

That plaintiff and the defendant became separated June 24th, 1949, and have lived separately and apart since said date when, although plaintiff was and has been a good true and dutiful wife towards the defendant, said defendant willfully abandoned and deserted plaintiff and has failed and refused to support her as his wife, without any just cause or legal excuse and which abandonment and desertion has been willful continuous and obstinate for a period of more than twelve months prior to the filing of this suit.

For as much therefore, as plaintiff is without an adequate remedy at law save in a court of equity she prays as follows:

A   That said defendant who is more than 21 years of age and a non resident of the State of Florida be served by publication in terms of the law.

B   That this Honorable Court grant unto plaintiff a divorce a vinculo matrimonii of and from the defendant.

_____
                    Attorney for plaintiff

State of Florida,
County of Hillsborough.

In person appeared before the undersigned authority, duly authorized by law to administer oaths, Vivian Edna Afeld, who on oath deposes and says that the facts set forth in the goregoingcomplaint are true.

Deponent further says that she has made diligent search and inquiry to ascertain the true name and residence of the defendant, her husband, Walter Eugene Afeld, and that same is set forth in this sworn statement as particlarly as is known to affiant; that said defendant above named is more than 21 years of age to affiant's knowledge and is a resident of a State or Country other than the State of Florida, namely, the State of New Jersey and that said defendant is a resident of Passaic, New Jersey, the exact street and address being unknown but that his Post office Box is 335, Passaic, N. J.

Vivian Edna Afeld

Sworn to and subscribed before me
Aug. 23rd, 1950.

Beatrice Foster Roberts

Notary Public, State of Florida at large
My commission expires March 16, 1953.
Bonded by Mass. Bonding & Insurance Co.

VIVIAN EDNA AFELD,

.... Plaintiff

vs.

WALTER EUGENE AFELD,

.... Defendant

No. 86576 C

Filed & Docketed

AUG 25 1950

CHAS H. PENT, Clerk

.... D. C.

NOTICE TO APPEAR

STATE OF FLORIDA:

TO Walter Eugene Afeld, whose residence is Passaic, New Jersey,

and whose mailing address is:

P.O. Box 335,

Passaic, New Jersey

You are hereby required to file your written defenses, if any ~~answer or answer~~ in the above proceeding in this Court on or before the 25th day of September 19 50 the nature of which proceeding being

A SUIT FOR DIVORCE

Done and ordered at Tampa Hillsborough County, State of Florida, this 25th day of August, 19 50 [Seal]

CHAS. H. PENT,
Clerk Circuit Court

By .... D. C.

Billie B. Bush
Solicitor for Plaintiff.

Walter failed to respond to the summons and the Court proceeded without him.

IN THE CIRCUIT COURT OF HILLSBOROUGH COUNTY FLORIDA.

VIVIAN EDNA AFELD

        Plaintiff

vs

WALTER EUGENE AFELD,

        Defendant.

No. 86576-C

Divorce

Filed & Docketed

SEP 25 1950

CHAS H. PE IT, Clerk

B_____ D.C.

Praecipe for decree pro confesso.

To the Clerk of the Above Styled Court:

The defendant Walter Eugene Afeld having failed to answer plaintiff's complaint as directed by this Court on September 25th, 1950, you will please enter a decree pro confesso against him according to law.

_____
Attorney for plaintiff

Having ignored all communication from the court, judgment was conferred upon Walter and a divorce was granted to Vivian.

IN THE CIRCUIT COURT OF HILLSBOROUGH COUNTY FLORIDA

VIVIAN EDNA AFELD,

Plaintiff.

Filed & Docketed

OCT 3 1950

CHAS. H. PENT, Clerk

By .... D. C.

No. 86576-C

DIVORCE.

vs.

WALTER EUGENE AFELD,

Defendant.

FINAL DECREE

This cause coming on regularly to be heard this day on the application of plaintiff, for a final decree and it appearing to the Court from an inspection of the record in said cause, consisting of the complaint of plaintiff, a decree pro confesso duly and legally entered against the defendant, and the testimony adduced before the Honorable Joseph Miyares, the duly appointed Special Master in said cause, together with his recommendations made therein, that this court has jurisdiction of the parties to this suit, and the subject matter thereof, and that the defendant, Walter Eugene Afeld, has been guilty of willfull, continuous and obstinate desertion of the plaintiff, Vivian Edna Afeld for a period of more than one year prior to the filing of this suit for divorce;

IT IS THEREFORE ORDERED ADJUDGED AND DECREED by the Court that the plaintiff, Vivian Edna Afeld, be and she is hereby granted a divorce a vinoulo matrimonii of and from the defendant, Walter Eugene Afeld, and the rights of each of said parties as single persons are hereby restored to each of them.

DONE IN CHAMBERS AT TAMPA FLORIDA, this October 3rd, 1950.

_____
JUDGE

Sometime between 1945 and 1949, Walter married Jeannette Garrette who operated a dance school in Brigantine, New Jersey. At this time, he was also still married to Vivian.

About Jeannette Garrette

Born on April 16, 1918, Chicago, Cook, Illinois, the daughter of George Gerymue Garrette and Jean Gremalar Inglas, a native of Toronto, Ontario, Canada. The family were performers who traveled widely. She enjoyed a successful performing career, stopping in 1952 to open a dance studio.

She purchased a home at 1804 Ocean Avenue, in Brigantine, New Jersey. None of the city directories that were located ever include Walter in the listing. Her dance studio – the Jeannette Garrette Studio of Dancing, was located at 1 South New Haven Avenue in Atlantic City.

Newspaper articles say that she married twice, but had no children. Her second husband was Frederick Porter, a native of Ontario, Canada, who died on February 15, 1999. (Ocean City Sentinal, vol. 118, no. 46, Feb. 25, 1999, page A2)

An Excerpt from Her Obituary

> **PORTER, JEANNETTE "Garrette",** 87 - of Linwood, ending her courageous battle with cancer, **Jeannette Porter**, known to her dance students as "Miss Garrette," passed away peacefully in her sleep on April 25, 2005, at home, with close friends by her side.

Jeannette was born on April 16, 1918, in Chicago, IL. She was the daughter of Jean and George Garrette. Together, they traveled Canada and the United States performing their vaudeville act, "The Dumbbells." Jeannette began her professional dance career at the age of four and was dubbed "The Canadian Shirley Temple".

Jeannette's dance career took her to Cuba, Radio City Music Hall in NY, and finally, to Atlantic City, where she began teaching contestants of the Miss America Pageant. On stage, Jeannette entertained alongside the likes of Billie Holiday, Dean Martin & Jerry Lewis, the Andrew Sisters, and many others. Jeannette owned and operated the Jeannette Garrette Dance Studio in Brigantine for many years before moving it to Linwood. More recently, she gave the studio, where she taught through her eighties, to a former student. It continues to operate today as the New Motion Dance Studio. (April 28, 2005, page C2, Copyright, 2005, South Jersey Publishing Company t/a The Press of Atlantic City.)

This is the last photograph taken of Walter Afeld before his death in 1956.

Walter died in on July 6, 1956, at the Normandy Hotel in San Juan, Puerto Rico. His son, Hollis, confirmed in a personal interview that his father was cremated and that he caste his ashes at a cemetery near their hometown in New Jersey.

Death Certificate of Walter Eugene Afeld. Registro Civil, 1836–2001. Digital images. Departamento de Salud de Puerto Rico, San Juan, Puerto Rico. Citing book 164, certificate number 674.

Third Generation

Hollis Walter Afield

Hollis was born on January 16, 1929 at Clifton, New Jersey. He graduated from Clifton High School in 1947. He attended Patterson State Teachers College between 1947 and 1949 and then transferred to University of Pennsylvania, where he studied economics and political science, graduating in 1951.

Upon graduation he was drafted into the U.S. Army Infantry and completed basic training at Fort Dix in New Jersey. While in the Army, he completed Radio Repair School at Fort Benning in Georgia and was assigned to the Signal Corp at Fort Meade in Maryland until his discharge in April 1953.

Following his discharge, Hollis decided to enter the hotel business. His first position was as a Clerk at the Sagamore Resort Hotel at Lake George, New York, during the summer of 1953. During this time period, many of the resort hotels were seasonal, catering to families interested in extended stays. So, Hollis worked in the north during the summer months and in Saint Petersburg at the Soreno Resort Hotel during the winter months. His mother and grandparents were retired and living in Saint Petersburg at the time.

Hollis at the Otesaga Resort Hotel in 1987, where he was General Manager.

In subsequent summers, Hollis worked at The Inn at Buck Hill Falls (1954), as a part of the management team, overseeing reservations and at Lake Minnewaska in New Paltz, New York (1955), and at Saranac Lake Resort in Saranac, New York (1956). He returned to Saint Petersburg each winter season.

He met his future wife, Mildred Morris, during the winter season in Saint Petersburg. Her parents, Julie and Charlie Morris, owned the Bluebird Inn Restaurant, a seasonal family restaurant in Franklin Lakes, New Jersey that operated from 1935 until 1960. The family wintered in Saint Petersburg. Hollis and Mildred married on May 7, 1957, at Ridgewood, New Jersey. They welcomed a baby girl, Barbara Holly Afield, to the world while residing in Princeton, New Jersey on February 5, 1958.

In July 1959, Hollis began working at the Bankers Trust Company in New York City, where he served as Food Service Manager through 1964. From there he moved into a position with the bank as Assistant Manager at 415 Madison Avenue branch. In 1972, he was appointed Assistant Treasurer of the bank and remained through 1974.

Mildred Morris Afield and Hollis at the Biltmore Estate in Asheville, North Carolina.

Hollis served as Assistant Vice President at Midland Bank in Paramus, New Jersey (1975-1977) and at New Jersey Bank in West Patterson, New Jersey from 1977 through 1980. In 1980, the family moved south, and Hollis returned to the Soreno Resort Hotel as Resident Manager and stayed until the hotel was closed in 1985.

In 1989, Hollis went to work for the U.S. Bureau of the Census and helped to enumerate the Twenty-First Census of the United States in April 1990. Following the census, Hollis was offered permanent employment with the Census Bureau enumerating the unemployment specialty census, which he did until his retirement in 1995.

Fourth Generation

Barbara Holly Afield was born on February 5, 1958 in New Jersey. She lives in Florida and is a CPA. She recently retired after a 27-year career with Duke Energy.

Chapter 7

The First Generation: Charles Oscar Richard Afeld

Oscar Frances Charles Richard Afeld was born on March 19, 1875 in Boston, Suffolk, Massachusetts, a son of Franz Wilhelm Afeld and Theresa Sandbichler. His name was registered as Oscar Frances. At some point before 1898, he began using Oscar Charles, and the use of Richard is only evident in his obituary and on his headstone.

BIRTHS REGISTERED IN THE CITY OF BOSTON					
REC #	DATE OF BIRTH	NAME OF CHILD		SEX	PLACE OF BIRTH
7891	March 19	Oscar	Frances	Afeld	M	9 Chapman

FATHER	MOTHER	RESIDENCE	OCCUPATION	PLACE OF BIRTH OF FATHER	OF MOTHER
Francis	Theresa	[Boston]	Artificial Flower	Germany	Germany

Massachusetts, Town and Vital Records, 1620-1988 [database on-line]. Provo, UT, USA. Original data: Town and City Clerks of Massachusetts. *Massachusetts Vital and Town Records*. Provo, UT: Holbrook Research Institute (Jay and Delene Holbrook).

Charles enlisted in the military on May 2, 1898 in New York City, New York. (Private; Company I, 9th Regiment, New York Infantry. Spanish American War. He received a medical discharge on October 31, 1898.). He applied for a military pension on ugust 6, 1927 (Pension Application #13-8834. Certificate #A 1-21-28) and was a member of Colonel John Jacob Astor's Camp No. 28, Veterans of the Spanish American War.

The 9th Regiment Infantry, New York Volunteers in the Spanish-American War

On April 25th, 1898 the United States of America declared war on Spain. On the 23rd of April, two days before the official declaration of war, President William McKinley issued a call for 125,000 volunteers to bolster the ranks of the regular U.S. Army for the coming conflict in the Philippines and the Caribbean.

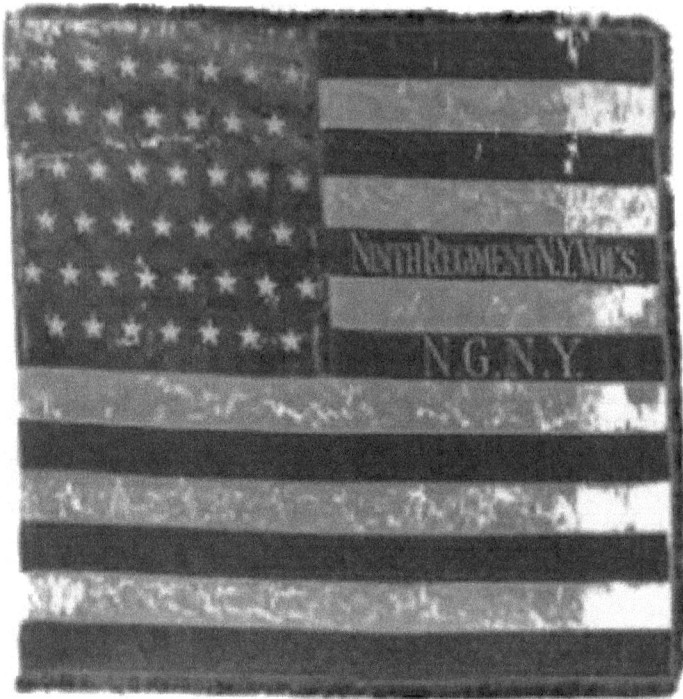

The 9th Infantry Regiment was one of twelve New York State National Guard infantry regiments that were federalized for service in the Spanish-American War. The 9th Regiment was officially organized in June of 1859 but some of its parent companies date back to the War of 1812. The regiment was entirely staffed by men from New York City and was actively called upon by the State of New York to deal with instances of unrest. Elements of the 9th Regiment was called to service during the abolition riots of 1835, the great fire in New York City of 1845, the Orange riot of 1871 and the three railroad riots of 1877, 1892, and 1895 at Albany, Buffalo, and Brooklyn respectively.

On May 3rd, 1898 the regiment was reorganized as a twelve-company unit and officially mustered into federal service as the "9th Regiment Infantry, New York Vols."

The 9th Regiment was mustered in at Camp Townsend, NY and departed on the 24th of May after several weeks of drill, bound for Camp George H. Thomas at Chickamauga Park in Tennessee. The regiment arrived on the 26th of May and by the 29th was officially attached to the First Brigade, of the Second Division, of the Third Army Corp., where it was brigaded with the 1st Arkansas and the 2nd Kentucky. The Regiment remained at Camp Thomas until September 13th when it was returned to New York and mustered out on November 15th, 1898 having never fired a shot. (Source: New York State Division of Military and Naval Affairs: Military History. URL: http://www.dmna.state.ny.us/historic).

Following his discharge, he returned to Manhattan and lived with his parents at 59 West 11th Street. In the 1900 US Federal Census, he indicates that he has been employed as a wood engraver for the previous 12 months.

On 12 September 1918, he completed a World War I Draft Registration card, which gives proof of his date of birth and the first record we have stating what would become his career, a letter carrier. The enrollment officer indicates that he is of medium height, medium build, and has blue eyes and brown hair. He resides at 560 Prospect Place in Brooklyn. He was not drafted for service.

Source Information: United States, Selective Service System. World War I Selective Service System Draft Registration Cards, 1917-1918. Washington, D.C.: National Archives and Records Administration. M1509, 4,582 rolls. Registration State: New York; Registration County: Kings; Roll: 1754392; Draft Board: 47.

Charles married Catherine C. Schadowski (aka Schade), daughter of Jacob Shadowski and Dorothea Grobe on November 28, 1931 in Cuyahoga, Ohio (by Rev. S.W. Wilson). She was born on November 18, 1894 in Cleveland, Cuyahoga, Ohio. Her parents immigrated from Germany in 1886. They shortened their surname to Schade sometime between 1910 and 1920.

```
NEW SERIES LICENSE NO. A 2389      FILED AND MARRIAGE LICENSE ISSUED      November 27      19 31
Name        Charles R.Afeld                          Name        Catharine C.Schade
Age    49    Residence    572 Prospect Pl.,           Age    37    Residence    3038 Packett Av.
Place of Birth    Boston,Mass.    /Brooklyn,N.Y.      Place of Birth                Cleveland
Occupation              Post Office                   Occupation
Father's Name          Franz W.Afeld                  Father's Name          Jacob Schade
Mother's Maiden Name   Theresa Sand                   Mother's Maiden Name   Dorothea Grobe
Number of times previously married    None            Number of times previously married        None
                                                      Married Name
Marriage to be solemnized by Rev.  Wilson,Trowbridge Rd. Application taken by    H.W.Beckman        Deputy Clerk
Consent of              Filed              19         Date of application    Nov. 27,1931
                                                      Consent of             Filed              19
                                                      License issued by      H.W.Beckman        Deputy Clerk
THE STATE OF OHIO, } ss.                              RETURN
  Cuyahoga County,
I CERTIFY, That on the 28th    day of  November       19  31 Mr.    Charles R.Afeld
  and Miss    Catharine C.Schade                      were by me legally joined in marriage.
                                                          Rev.  S.W.Wilson
```

(Source: Cuyahoga County Archive; Cleveland, Ohio; Cuyahoga County, Ohio, Marriage Records, 1810-1973; Volume: Vol 165-166; Page: 478; Year Range: 1931 Jun - 1932 Jan.)

The couple resided at 250 Chase Avenue in Lakewood until the death of Charles. He died at his home on July 11, 1961 in Lakewood, Cuyahoga, Ohio. (Death Certificate: 47504; Volume: 16577). He was buried at Calvary Cemetery (section 63) on July 14, 1961.

Obituary

O. Charles Richard Afeld, *beloved husband of Catherine (nee Schade), brother of Mrs. Amelia Marshall of Matawan, N. J. Tuesday, July 11, 1961, residence, 250 Chase Ave. Friends may call Thursday, 3-5 and 7-9:30 p.m. at McGorray Bros. Lakewood Home, 14133 Detroit Ave. Funeral mass*

*Friday, July 14, St. Luke Church (Clifton and Bunts Rd.), at 10 a.m.
Interment Cavalry Cemetery. Member of Col. John Jacob Astor Camp
No. 28. New York Spanish-American War Veterans. Kindly omit flowers.
(Source: Cleveland Press, July 13, 1961. Extracted from Cleveland
Necrology File, reel #89; Cleveland Public Library, Cleveland, Ohio.)*

Charles and Catherine did not have any children.

Fourteen years later, Catherine married Michael M. Letich on April 5, 1975
in Cleveland, Ohio. He was born about 1894 in Hamburg, Germany. He
was a widower and a member of her church, St. Luke's. He died on
January 21, 1983 in Cleveland, Cuyahoga, Ohio, at age 89.

Catherine died at age 84 on February 4, 1979 in Lakewood, Cuyahoga,
Ohio. She was buried next to Charles at Calvary Cemetery on February 7,
1979.

Obituary

Catherine C. Letich (Afeld) (nee Schade), *beloved wife of Micahel M.,
sister of the late Mary Downes McGreavey, Elizabeth Bromeler, Paul,
Albert, Charles, Frank, and Anna Twining and Gertrude Bayne. Sunday,
Feb. 4, 1979. Funeral Mass Wednesday Feb. 7, St. Luke Church, Clifton
and Bunts Rd. at 9:30 a.m. Interment Calvary Cemetery. Friends may call
at The McGorray Funeral Home, 14133 Detroit Ave., Tuesday 3-5 and 7-9
p.m. (Source: Plain Dealer, Cleveland, Ohio. February 6, 1979, section C,
page 7.)*

Chapter 8

The First Generation: Amelia Afeld

Amelia Afeld was born on March 11, 1877 in Boston, Massachusetts, the daughter of Franz and Theresa Sandbichler Afeld. In 1898, she married Frederick William Marshall. The newlyweds lived in a rented apartment in Passaic, New Jersey, and welcomed their first child into the world in December 1898.

By 1910, the family had moved to Brooklyn and resided at 56 Morgan Avenue. The census records indicate that they owned the residence with a mortgage. Frederick was employed as a manager in the "Ice Business."

In 1920, the family has grown significantly with nine children in the household. They live in a rented home at 66 Tuers Avenue, in Jersey City. Frederick is employed as a "printer" at a publishing house. Their oldest son, Arthur (age 16), is recorded with the same occupation and their daughter, Florence (age 14), is recorded with an occupation of "paster" at a pocket book factory (pasting layout copy for paperback books).

In 1930, Frederick, Amelia and six children reside at 390 High Street in Jersey City in a rented home. The family owns a radio, a question asked in preparedness for national emergencies and as a byproduct of communication during World War I. Frederick is still employee as a printer and Amelia is a homemaker. Sons Harold and Lester are working in a clerical role at a magazine.

The 1940 U.S. Federal Census was the first record of the condition of the citizens coming out of the Great Depression. It sought to look at migration and employment data in greater detail. It asked where the family resided in 1935 and in 1940. In the case of Frederick and Amelia, they resided at

(L-R) Amelia with daughters Evelyn, Mildred and Dorothy at the beach.

274 Virginia Avenue in Jersey City in a rented home valued at $2,500 in 1940. They indicated that they had moved from a prior residence in 1935, but remained in Jersey City.

While this appears relatively normal, it is obvious that the family struggled with employment. Frederick indicated that he was a "printer" and had been unemployed for the previous 42 weeks, reporting a total income of $643.35 for the prior 12 months ($10,703 in 2014 dollars). Their son, Harold, a construction laborer, indicated that he had been without work for 72 weeks. Their son, Ralph, was employed as a "platform worker" for the railroad. He indicated that he worked about 24 hours in the prior week and that his wages for the prior year were $1,360 ($22,639 in 2014 dollars). Two sisters, Mildred and Dorothy, were also in the household with no occupation listed.

In an interview with Amelia's granddaughter, Leslie, she described her as, "stoic, strong-willed, and tough." She loved to play cards, bingo, and was "an ace at flipping spoons across the room." She remembers her spending more time with her granddaughters than her grandsons and, also, remembers her tying rags in her daughters hair at bedtime so they would have curls in the morning.

Amelia Afeld Marshall, Frederick Marshall and their granddaughter.

Frederick died in September 1942 at age 69. Amelia died in 1971 at Matawan, New Jersey, at age 94.

The images below are from a journal kept by Amelia (currently in possession of her granddaughter, Leslie) and are in her handwriting. While it is clear that some of the entries are made around the date of their occurrence, some are written at the same time. It is also worth noting that some of the dates differ from those used by her children and found in public records.

Father of Amelia

Franz Wilhelm Afeld
died November 2 — 1904
78 years old

Mother of Amelia

Theresa Afeld mother
died Oct 27 — 1926
78 years old

Brother

Eugene Afeld brother
died Feb 8 — 1947
age 78 years

Sister

Norma Evans sister
died Dec 1 — 1924
age

Birthdays

Fredrick	Dec. 3	1898
Herbert	Oct. 11	1900
Arthur	Jan. 1	1902
Florence	Feb. 8	1905
Walter	March 1	1907
Edna	May. 26	1908
Lester	Dec. 26	1910
Harold	Dec. 4	1912
Ralph	April. 16	1915
Evelyn	Dec. 7	1917
Mildred	June 9	1919
Dorothy	Mar. 10	1921
Amelia	Mar. 11	1878

Died

Mr Fredrick Marshall
Sept 29 — 1942
69 years old

Brother

Chas Afeld
1250 Chase Ave
Lakewood 7
Ohio

Norma died Monday
Dec 1 1924

Eugene Afeld died
Feb 8th 1947 age 78

Mother Died Afeld
Oct 27, 1926 Age 78

Fredrick Marshall
died Sept 29 1942

Herbert Marshall
Died June 9 — 1910
9 years 6 month

Edna Marshall
died 1

Walter Marshall died
Friday March 16 — 1923
16 years old

Mildred Marshall died
November 18 1952
age 33 years

99

The Descendants of Amelia Afeld and Frank Marshall

How to follow this outline: When a **(#)** appears before a name, look for that number in the next generation for their marriage and children.

Frederick Marshall and Amelia Afeld had the following children:

1. Frederick J. Marshall was born on December 3, 1898 in New York.

2. Herbert Marshall was born on October 11, 1900 in Passaic, Passaic, New Jersey. He died on June 5, 1910.

3. **(3)** Arthur Marshall was born January 1, 1902 in New Jersey.

4. **(4)** Florence N. Marshall was born on February 8, 1905 in Jersey City, New Jersey. She died on August 4, 1982 in Holmdel, Monmouth, New Jersey.

5. Walter Marshall was born on March 1, 1907 in New Jersey. He died on March 16, 1923 in New Jersey.

6. Edna Marshall was born on May 26, 1908 in New Jersey.

7. **(7)** Lester Marshall was born on December 26, 1910 in Jersey City, Hudson, New Jersey. He died on December 17, 1979 in Lincroft, Monmouth, New Jersey.

8. **(8)** Harold Marshall was born on December 4, 1912 in New Jersey. He died on January 1, 1996 in Keyport, Monmouth, New Jersey.

9. Raymond "Ralph" Marshall was born on April 16, 1915 in New Jersey. He died on March 2, 1963 in Ringoes, Hunterdon, New Jersey. He married Elizabeth O'Connor.

10. **(10)** Evelyn Marshall was born on December 7, 1916 in Jersey City, Hudson, New Jersey. She died on March 29, 2009 in Mount Airy, Habersham, Georgia at age 92.

11. Mildred Marshall was born on 09 Jun 1918 in New Jersey. She died on 18 Nov 1952 in New Jersey.

12. **(12)** Dorothy Marshall was born on March 10, 1921 in Jersey City, Hudson, New Jersey. She died on February 8, 1979 in Jersey City, Hudson, New Jersey.

13. Baby Marshall, stillborn, 1923.

Generation 2

(3) Arthur Marshall was born on January 1, 1902 in New Jersey. He married Clara who was born about 1906 in New York.

Arthur Marshall and Clara had the following children:
- Clara Marshall was born about 1925 in New Jersey.
- Arthur Marshall was born about 1926 in New Jersey.
- Barbara Marshall was born about 1937 in New Jersey.
- Fred Marshall was born about 1938 in New Jersey.

(4) Florence N. Marshall was born on February 8, 1905 in Jersey City, New Jersey. She died on August 4, 1982 in Holmdel, Monmouth, New Jersey. She married Douglas Leslie Taylor who was born about 1906 in New Jersey. He died in 1958.

Douglas Leslie Taylor and Florence N. Marshall had the following children:
- **(14)** Robert Taylor was born in 1930 in New Jersey.
- Douglas Taylor was born in 1932 in Jersey City.

Florence Marshall.

(7) Lester Marshall was born on December 26, 1910 in Jersey City, Hudson, New Jersey. He died on December 17, 1979 in Lincroft, Monmouth, New Jersey at age 69. He married Margaret VanDorn Gillingham who was born on August 21, 1913 in New Jersey. She died on September 13, 2004 in Holmdell, New Jersey.

Lester Marshall and Margaret Gillingham had the following children:

Lester Marshall.

- **(15)** Margaret Leslie Marshall was born in New Jersey on July 13, 1941.
- **(16)** Thomas Marshall was born on March 2, 1945.
- Pamela Ann Marshall was born on November 3, 1953 in New Jersey.

(8) Harold Marshall was born on December 4, 1912 in New Jersey. He died in January 1996 in Keyport, Monmouth, New Jersey. He married Catherine Haggerty.

Harold Marshall and Catherine Haggerty had the following children:
(17) Patricia Mary Marshall who was born on July 5, 1943 in New Jersey.
- Harold William Marshall was born on September 1, 1949 in New Jersey.

Harold Marshall with his wife, Catherine "Kay" at the beach.

(10) Evelyn Marshall was born on December 7, 1916 in Jersey City, Hudson, New Jersey. She died on March 29, 2009 in Mount Airy, Habersham, Georgia at age 92. She married John William Allen who was born on January 6, 1916 in New York City, New York. He died on February 16, 1976 in Pemberton, Burlington, New Jersey.

The Allen Family: Front row: John, Kenneth, Raymond, and Harold. Back row: Evelyn Marshall Allen and John William Allen.

John William Allen and Evelyn Marshall had the following children:
- John Allen born about 1936 in New Jersey.

- **(18)** Kenneth Allen was born on September 21, 1937.
- Harold F. Allen was born on February 19, 1940 in Jersey City, Hudson, New Jersey. He died on March 5, 1997 in Columbia, Boone, Missouri.
- Raymond Allen was born on February 17, 1942.

(12) Dorothy Marshall was born on March 10, 1921 in Jersey City, Hudson, New Jersey. She died on February 8, 1979 in Jersey City, New Jersey. She married Frank Robert MacDonald Jr. who was born on August 7, 1920. He died on January 8, 1985 in Jersey City, Hudson, New Jersey.

Left-to-right: Evelyn Marshall, Amelia Afeld Marshall, Frank McDonald and Dorothy Marshall McDonald.

Frank MacDonald Jr. and Dorothy Marshall had the following children:
- **(19)** Robert Frank MacDonald was born on October 6, 1941 in Jersey City, Hudson, New Jersey.
- **(20)** Russell MacDonald was born on May 26, 1948 in New Jersey.

Additional Photos from Generation 2

Evelyn Marshall.

Tom Marshall, Florence Marshall Taylor, Leslie Marshall.

Pam Marshall, Leslie Marshall, Dorothy Marshall McDonald, Frank McDonald and Russell McDonald about 1958.

Mildred Marshall.

Generation 3

(14) Robert Taylor was born about 1930 in New Jersey. He married Elizabeth Saez.

Robert Taylor and Elizabeth Saez had the following child:

- Linda Lee Taylor
- Leslie Douglas Taylor

Margaret Leslie Marshall with her grandmother, Amelia, and her brother, Thomas Marshall about 1949.

(15) Margaret Leslie Marshall was born on July 13, 1941.

She married:
(1) William Edward Ferinden Jr. was born on June 8, 1937. He died on June 30, 1973.
(2) Joseph E. Labatch, who was born on May 18, 1935 and died on August 27, 1989.
(3) Marshall Olds Culver, born July 30, 1933. He died on August 24, 1999.
(4) Gilfred Boyd Swartz. He was born on May 23, 1938.

William Ferinden Jr. and Leslie Marshall had the following children:
- **(21)** Dana Margaret Ferinden was born on September 8, 1963. She married John Luciano in 1989.
- **(22)** Laura Joan Ferinden was born on April 6, 1965.
- **(23)** William Edward Ferinden III was born on December 1, 1966.

Joseph E. LaBatch and Leslie Marshall had the following child:
- **(24)** Justine Florence Labatch was born on April 26, 1977.

(16) Thomas F. Marshall was born on March 2, 1945. He married Ugean Jo.
Thomas F. Marshall and Ugean Jo had the following children:
- Jemma Brynne Marshall was born on January 16, 1997.
- Jessie Marshall was born on July 18, 1999.
- Jared Marshall was born in February 2001.

(17) Patricia Mary Marshall was born on July 5, 1943 in New Jersey. She died on September 21, 1974 in New Jersey. She married Mr. Drobish.
Mr. Drobish and Patricia Mary Marshall had the following children:
- Robert Drobish
- Stacey Drobish

(18) Kenneth Allen was born on September 21, 1937. He married Edna who was born on May 21, 1941 in Secaucus, Hudson, New Jersey.
Kenneth Allen and Edna had the following children:
- Kenneth Allen Jr. was born on August 21, 1965.
- Cheryl Ann Allen was born on February 21, 1970. She married Richard Joseph Forziati.

(19) Robert Frank MacDonald was born on October 6, 1941 in Jersey City, Hudson, New Jersey. He married Mary Jane Ward who was born on

November 12, 1946 in Jefferson City, Jefferson, Tennessee.

Robert Frank MacDonald and Mary Jane Ward had the following children:

- Kristi MacDonald was born on December 21, 1969 in New Jersey.
- Heather Mary MacDonald was born on July 19, 1974 in New Jersey.

(20) Russell MacDonald was born on May 26, 1948 in New Jersey. He married Andrea Davis.

Russell MacDonald and Andrea Davis had the following children:

- Jennifer MacDonald was born on April 29, 1968.
- Laura MacDonald was born on October 17, 1969.
- Suzanna MacDonald was born on September 20, 1972.
- Erika MacDonald was born on December 12, 1974.

Generation 4

(21) Dana Margaret Ferinden was born on September 8, 1963. She married John Luciano in 1989.

Dana Margaret Ferinden and John Luciana had the following child:

- Marlene Margaret Luciano born on May 15, 1994.

(22) Laura Joan Ferinden was born on April 6, 1965. Laura had the following child:

- Frank William Mendes born on May 23, 1993.

She married Michael Deblasi.

Michael DeBlasi and Laura Joan Ferinden had the following child:

- Michael Anthony Deblasi born on September 23, 2000.

(23) William Edward Ferinden III was born in December 1966. He married Sheila McCarthy.

William Edward Ferinden III and Sheila McCarthy had the following child:

- Casey Lynn Ferinden was born on December 29, 2005.

(24) Justine Florence Labatch was born on April 26, 1977. She married Joseph Wenkelried. She married Chris Weber.

Joseph Wenkelried and Justine LaBatch had the following children:

- Madison Laura Wenkelried.
- Morgan Dana Wenkelried.

Chapter 9

The First Generation: Norma Julia Afeld

Norma Julia Afeld was born in July 1878 in Philadelphia, Pennsylvania. Her father, Franz, had relocated the family there from Boston, in order to promote the family artificial flower business in New York. The family moved back to New York City around 1880 and missed the enumeration of the 1880 US Census.

The next record we find for Norma is her marriage to Benjamin Gregg Evans on July 7, 1900, in Manhattan, New York.

Marriage record of Benjamin Evans and Norma Afeld, New York City Department of Records, Municipal Archives, New York, New York. Certificate number 11428.

About Benjamin's Family

Benjamin was born on October 7, 1875 in Flint River, Iowa, the son of Joseph H. Evans and Sarah Jane Gregg. A native of Virginia, Joseph was farming in Iowa as early as 1850. After the death of his first wife, Elizabeth Course, he married Sarah Gregg in 1874. Joseph fought in the Civil War for the Union. He is recorded in the 31st Regiment, Iowa Infantry, Company G. He enlisted as a Private and was successful in advancing to the rank of Captain at the time of his discharge. (National Park Service. U.S. Civil War Soldiers, 1861-1865 [database on-line]. Provo, UT, USA: Ancestry.com Operations Inc, 2007.)

On December 7, 1901, Norma and Benjamin welcomed their daughter, Norma Gregg Evans into the world.

About 1906, the family moved to Los Angeles, where Benjamin is employed as a Manager at a restaurant. Norma's mother, Theresa Sandbichler Afeld, is also enumerated at their residence and stayed with them until 1918, when she moved back to New York City.

Benjamin died on May 24, 1919. In 1920, Norma and her daughter are living in a rented residence at 720 West 42nd Street in Los Angeles. She is recorded in the US Census with an occupation of "Private Chauffer" and her daughter is working in clerical support at Western Union.

Norma died on December 1, 1924, in Los Angeles, California, at the age of 46.

Descendants of Norma Julia Afeld

Second Generation

Norma Gregg Evans

Norma Gregg Evans married Robert Benjamin Hallock on July 3, 1921 at Long Beach, California. Robert is a policeman for the City of Los Angeles. In 1940, the family resides at 10017 Town Avenue in Los Angeles. Robert reported a salary of $2,400. That's about $41,000 in present day currency.

About Robert and His Family

Robert was born on December 4, 1897 at Mulhall, Logan, Iowa to Noah Jason and Nora Hallock. By 1910, the family had moved to Los Angeles and owned a home at 762 East 50th Street. His father was in "iron worker" and his mother a "homekeeper". Robert had three sisters, Gertrude, Grace and Opal, and one younger brother, Myron.

All of the Hallock family is interred at Inglewood Cemetery Park in Inglewood, California (720 East Florence Avenue, Inglewood, CA. Section: Sequoia, Lot 394). Further details about them may be seen by visiting the website (www.Findagrave.com). You can search by name or enter one of the memorial numbers listed below. The memorials of all of Robert's siblings and extended family are linked within the profiles.

Memorial #   Ancestor
57275711   Noah Jason Hallock (Father of Robert)
115742070   Nora Isabell *Fleener* Hallock (Mother of Robert)
115755939   Robert Bejamin Hallock (Son of Noah and Nora)
78712190   Norma Gregg Evans Hallock (daughter of Norma Afeld)
115756975   Allen Dion Hallock (Son of Robert and Norma)

Robert died on January 1, 1956 at Apple Valley, California and Norma Gregg Evans died on June 13, 1984 at Sunnyvale, California. They were the parents of at least two children, Robert and Allen.

Third Generation

Robert D. Hallock

Robert was born on August 20, 1924 in Los Angeles, California (State of California. *California Birth Index, 1905-1995*. Sacramento, CA, USA: State of California Department of Health Services, Center for Health Statistics.).

He enlisted in the U.S. Army on March 24, 1943. His enlistment papers indicate that he completed four years of high school and had been employed as a "Machinists apprentice". (World War II Army Enlistment Records; Records of the National Archives and Records Administration, Record Group 64; National Archives at College Park. College Park, Maryland).

The records indicate that he survived the War, as several city directory listings place him in the Sunnyvale, California area as late as 1996. No further information was located.

Allen Dion Hallock

Allen was born on May 3, 1933 in Los Angeles, California (State of California. *California Birth Index, 1905-1995*. Sacramento, CA, USA: State of California Department of Health Services, Center for Health Statistics.). He married Louise M. Barrs on April 27, 1957 at Las Vegas, Clark County, Nevada. (Nevada, Marriage Index, 1956-2005 [database on-line]. Provo, UT, USA: Ancestry.com Operations, Inc., 2007.)

Allen died on July 6, 1985. From his death notice in the *Los Angeles Times*, we learn that he was a longtime employee with the Hollywood Park Race Track and that he was a father and uncle. There are undoubtedly additional descendants of this line still living on the west coast. Generally, it becomes harder to track individuals after World War II. The Census records for 1950 to present have not been released and people have become more mobile.

Chapter 10

The Sandbichler Family of Bavaria, Germany

The Sandbichler family arrived at the Port of New York on July 16, 1867 aboard the Steamship Atlantic. The ship departed from Bremen and made one stop at Southampton before crossing. In the passenger manifest, Benedick gives his occupation as "mechanician", which is an old term for à mechanical engineer. This would support their ability to all travel at once in second class cabins, rather than in smaller groups and in third class, which was common for most immigrant families. Given that the eldest child traveling with them was 18 years old and allowing for Maria's age, it is possible that older children remained in Germany.

Of note, two entries prior to the Sandbichler family is Joseph Gerber, a 26-year old musician, who eventually marries Adeline Sandbichler and who is also found as one of the witnesses on the marriage license of Franz Afeld and Theresa Sandbichler. Either he knew them in Germany or became friends with them during the voyage to New York.

Passenger Manifest of the Steamship Atlantic

National Archives Microfilm Serial: M237, 1820-1897; Microfilm Roll: Roll 283; Lines: 31-40; List Number: 735.

Benedick Maximilian Sandbichler	Maria Mary Staeger
Born: 1820 Bavaria, Germany	Born: Abt. 1822 Bavaria, Germany
Died: Abt. 1884 New York City, New York	Died: Bef. 1881 New York

Marriage:

Children:	Sex	Birth	Death
Maria Sandbichler	F	Abt. 1849 Germany	Bef. 1898 New York
Maximilian Sandbichler	M	Abt. 1850 Munich, Bavaria, Germany	
Theresa Sandbichler	F	30 Aug 1850 Gmund, Bavaria, Germany	20 Oct 1926 Brooklyn, Kings, New York
Adeline Sandbichler	F	Abt. 1851 Bavaria, Germany	
Jeremiah Sandbichler	M	Abt. 1854 Bavaria, Germany	
Siegmund Sandbichler	M	1856 Bavaria, Germany	23 Apr 1898 Brooklyn, Kings, New York
Bertha L. Sandbichler	F	Abt. 1858 Munich, Bavaria, Germany	

The Sandbichler Name

Older European names can often be dissected to help tease out their origin. The practice of maintaining a common surname didn't come into play until the late 15th century unless you were a member of the nobility. More often, you were identified by your name, occupation and location. In applying that to the name Sandbichler, we get a rough translation of the baker (German name bichler) on Sand Street. Since we know that Benedick was an engineer, the origin of the name would perhaps have applied to his grandfather or great grandfather.

However, the family name immediately came to an end after Benedick disembarked at New York. He immediately shortened the family name to Sand and you'll see either Sand or Sands in most of the historical public records.

The family is first enumerated in the 1870 US Census where Benedick has taken a job as a Life Insurance salesman. Max Jr. is employed in the artificial flower industry, most likely that of the Afeld family.

Surname	Given Name	Age	Birth Year	Gender	Race	Occupation	Value of Personal Estate	Birthplace
Sands	Benedick M.	50	1820	Male	White	Life Insurance Agent		Bavaria
Sands	Mary	40	1830	Female	White	Keeping House		Bavaria
Sands	Max	22	1848	Male	White	Manufacture of Artificial Flowers	1000	Bavaria
Sands	Mary	20	1850	Female	White	Manufacture of Caps	200	Bavaria
Sands	Adeline	19	1851	Female	White			Bavaria
Sands	Theresa	18	1852	Female	White			Bavaria
Sands	Sigmund	17	1853	Male	White			Bavaria
Sands	Bertha	15	1855	Female	White			Bavaria

Source Citation: Year: 1870; Census Place: New York Ward 15 District 4, New York, New York; Roll: M593_993; Page: 489B; Image: 234; Family History Library Film: 552492.

On October 14, 1875, Benedick becomes a Naturalized citizen the United States. He is the only member of the family for which a naturalization record was located.

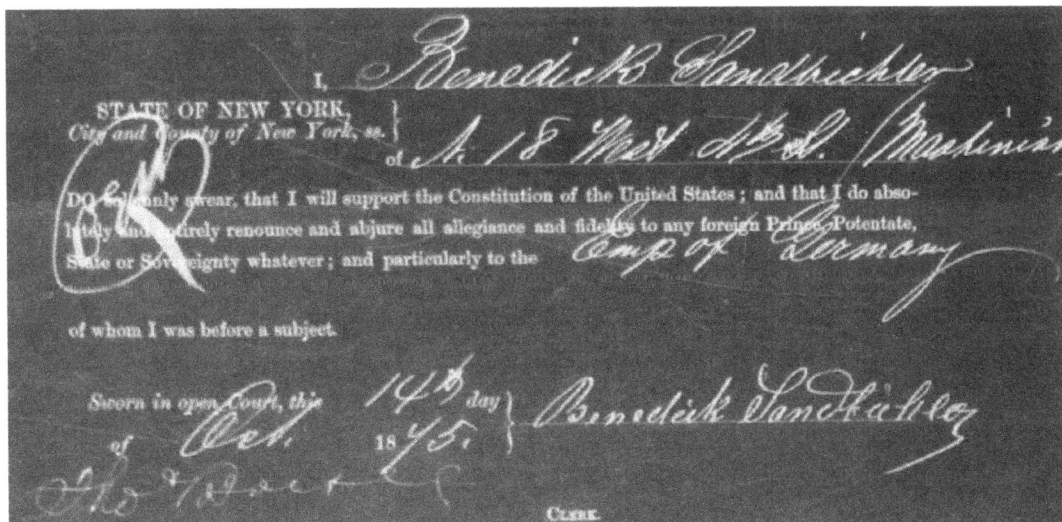

Source: National Archives at New York City; Superior Court of the City of New York (265-266); ARC Number: 5324244; Petitions for Naturalization, 1793-1906; Record Group Title: Records of the Immigration and Naturalization Service; Record Group Number: 85.

1880 US Federal Census

Census records can tell us a great deal about a family. This record is also an example of how many errors can occur, either by the person who provides the information, the recording of the census taker, or in the transcription of the records 75 years later by volunteers.

In this census, three generations are under the same roof and they have recently lost the matriarch, Maria Staeger Sandbichler. The family is doing well financially as is evidenced by the presence of three household servants. Most of the family is working in the artificial flower business, either at the shop or the manufacturing facility. Additional fields of information are available on the original document.

Line	Surname	Given Name	Age	Relationship	Marital Status	Occupation	Birthplace
1	Sands	Marks	57	Self	Widower	Artificial Flower	Bavaria
2	Sands	Marks	33	Son	Single	Artist	Bavaria
3	Sands	Jeremiah	26	Son	Single	Artificial Flower	Bavaria
4	Sands	Sarah	24	Daughter	Single	Artificial Flower	Kentucky
5	Rothriquec	Bertha	24	Daughter	Single	Artificial Flower	Bavaria
6	Rothriquec	Ella	7	Grand-daughter	Single	At School	New York
7	Rothriquec	Paul	1	Grandson	Single		New York
8	Gerber	Joseph	34	Son-in-law	Married	Music Professor	Bavaria
9	Gerber	Adele	30	Daughter	Married	Keeping House	Bavaria
10	Gerber	Rudolph	2	Grandson	Single		New York
11	Isnir	Adele	26	Servant	Single	Servant	Alsace
12	Meyer	Anna	34	Servant	Single	Servant	Germany
13	Meyer	Christena	25	Servant	Single	Servant	Switzerland
14	Rothriquec	Francis	34	Boarder	Single	Boarder	Cuba
15	Deutzman	Mayer	35	Boarder	Single	Boarder	Germany

Line	Notes and Clarifications
1	This is Benedick Maxwell Sandbichler Sr.
2	This is Benedick Maxwell Sandbichler Jr., who went by "Max" his entire life.
3	This is Jeremiah Sandbichler, son of Benedick and Maria.
4	This is Sarah Fenchtwanger, daughter-in-law of Benedick and wife of Sigmund Sandbichler. She must have been at the residence when the census taker visited because she is also enumerated with her husband, living at her mother's home.
5	This is Bertha Sandbichler. She married Joseph Rodriguez, an Cuban immigrant. She is a widow at this time, even though the record states she is single.
6	Ella is the daughter of Bertha and Joseph.
7	Paul is the son of Bertha and Joseph.
8	Joseph was on the ship with the family and is now husband of Adeline Sandbichler.
9	This is Adeline Sandbichler, daughter of Benedick and Maria, and husband of Joseph.
10	Son of Joseph and Adeline.
11	Household servant of the Sandbichler family.
12	Household servant of the Sandbichler family.
13	Household servant of the Sandbichler family.
14	Francis is the brother-in-law of Bertha Rodriguez, brother to deceased Joseph.
15	Unknown relationship to the family.

Source Citation: Year: 1880; Census Place: New York City, New York, New York; Roll: 874; Family History Film: 1254874; Page: 436D; Enumeration District: 157; Images: 0035 and 0036.

Benedick and Maria were able to experience many joys during their lifetimes in New York, including the marriages of their children and the birth of eight grandchildren:

- Theresa to Franz Afeld in 1872, followed by the births of five grandchildren, Eugene, Norman, Oscar, Amelia and Norma.
- Adeline to Joseph Gerber and the birth of their first child, Rudolph in 1878.
- Sigmund to Sarah Fenchtwagner in 1878.
- Bertha to Joseph Rodriguez, followed by two grandchildren, Ella and Paul.

Maria died sometime before June of 1880 when the US Census enumerated Benedick as a widower. Benedick likely died between 1883 and 1884, last appearing in the 1884 New York City Directory. No death record was located for either.

Below are a few documents pertaining to their children.

Marriage of Bertha Sanbichler to Joseph Rodriguez in 1894.

TO THE BUREAU OF VITAL STATISTICS,

Metropolitan Board of Health, State of New York.

RETURN OF A MARRIAGE.

1. Full Name of HUSBAND, *Joseph Rodriguez*
2. Place of Residence, *69 Washington St.*
3. Age next Birthday *27* years,
4. *Wh.*
5. Occupation, *Tailor*
6. Place of Birth, *Antonies — Spain*
7. Father's Name, *Joseph Rodriguez*
8. Mother's Maiden Name, *Jane Suendez*
9. No. of Husband's Marriage, *first*
10. Full Name of WIFE, *Bertha Sanbichler*
    Maiden Name, if a Widow,
11. Place of Residence, *69 — Washington St.*
12. Age next birthday, *19* years,
13. *W*
14. Place of Birth, *Muenchen Bavaria*
15. Father's Name, *Benedict Sandbichler*
16. Mother's Maiden Name, *Maria nee Hagn*
17. No. of Wife's Marriage, *first*

N. B.—At Nos. 4 and 13 state if Colored; if other races specify what. At Nos. 9 and 17 state whether 1st, 2d, 3d, &c., Marriage of each.

Church   New York, *June 28th* 1894

We, the Husband and Wife named in the above Certificate, hereby Certify that the information given is correct, to the best of our knowledge and belief.

Joseph Rodriguez (Husband.)
Bertha Sandbichler (Wife.)

Signed in presence of *Max Sandbichler*
and *Joseph Gerbel.*

Marriage of Bertha Sandbichler and Joseph Rodriguez. New York City Municipal Archives.

In 1898, apparently after the death of both his sister Maria (aka Mary Sandbichler) and his wife Sarah, Sigmund committed suicide.

DEAD ON HIS WIFE'S GRAVE.

Sigmund Sand Shot Himself in Mount Hope Cemetery.

The dead body of Sigmund Sand, a middle-aged German, was found yesterday on the grave of his wife, in Mount Hope Cemetery, Borough of Queens. The cemetery is just beyond the border of Brooklyn, and the cemetery employe who found the body, Frank Seifert, notified the police of the Liberty Avenue Station in that borough, who removed it to Deininger's undertaking establishment, Liberty and Miller Avenues.

Sand had shot himself in the right temple with a Colt's revolver of heavy calibre, which was clutched in his hand when he was found. He had been dead for probably twenty-four hours. In his pockets were found two braids of dark brown hair in envelopes, one marked " My wife, Sarah," and the other, " My sister, Maria." There was also a letter in German, reading as follows:

Dear Mother, Sister, and Brother: I bid you all farewell. I wish my body cremated when I die.   SIGMUND.

P. S.—I give my watch, chain, and ring to my sister. I have no debts or enemies. Sister, brother, and friends, I wish you all to live happily.

Source: New York Times (1857-1922); Apr 25, 1898; page 7.

Marriage of Maximillian Sandbichler Jr. and Lydia Grunmann in 1880.

To the Bureau of Vital Statistics,

Health Department of the City of New York.

RETURN OF A MARRIAGE.

1. *Full Name of* GROOM, *Maximilian Sand.*
2. *Place of Residence,* 14 - N. 4th St.
3. *Age next Birthday,* 25 *years,*
4. —
5. *Occupation,* Painter
6. *Place of Birth,* Munich Bavaria
7. *Father's Name,* Benedict Sand.
8. *Mother's Maiden Name,* Marie née Steger
9. *No. of Groom's Marriage,* first
10. *Full Name of* BRIDE, Lydia Grundman
    Maiden Name, if a Widow, —
11. *Place of Residence,* 225 - 5th St.
12. *Age next Birthday,* 21 *years,*
13. White
14. *Place of Birth,* Dresden - Saxonia
15. *Father's Name,* Eduard Grundman
16. *Mother's Maiden Name,* Thereson Senler
17. *No. of Bride's Marriage,* first

N. B.—At Nos. 4 and 13 state if Colored : If of other races, specify what ? At Nos. 9 and 17 state whether 1st, 2d, 3d, &c., Marriage of each.

New York, 31st Nov. 18 80

We, the Groom and Bride named in the above Certificate, hereby Certify that the information given is correct, to the best of our knowledge and belief.

Maximilian Sand (Groom.)

Lydia Grunman (Bride.)

Signed in presence of Benedickt Sand,

and Adele Serbel

Frank Rodriguez

Marriage of Maximillian Sandbichler and Lydia Grumann. New York City Municipal Archives.

Chapter 11

The Ancestry of Anna Maria Drinnenberg of Hünfeld, Germany

My Great Great Grandmother

Anna Maria Drinnenberg

Much of what we know about the Drinnenberg, Klüber, Köhler and Marschall family lines in Germany is simply dates of birth, christening, marriage and death that come from the church records. In several instances, clerics chose to reveal small bits of information that enable us to provide some color or historical context to their lives as you'll see in this branch of the family tree.

This chapter is split into two sections – her father's line and her mother's line and the entries progress from youngest to oldest under each line and all shown relationships are to Walter Afield who commissioned this book. All of the church records in this chapter are from the Diocesan Archives of the Diocese of Fulda (Paulustor 5, D-36037 Fulda. Web: www.katholische-archive.de/Diözesanarchive/Fulda).

Her Father's Line – Drinnenberg and Klüber

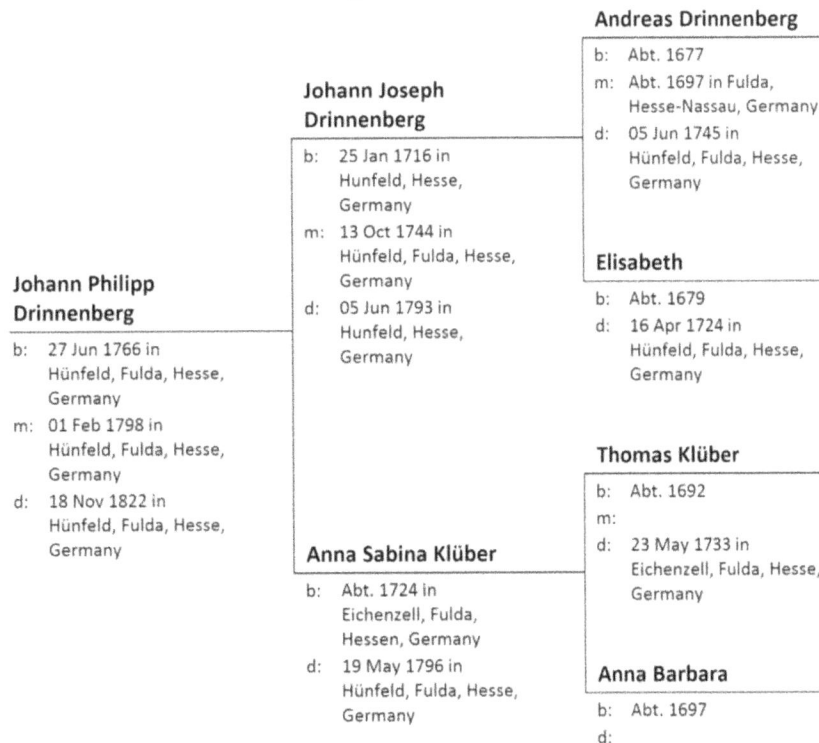

Johann Philipp Drinnenberg

b: 27 Jun 1766 in Hünfeld, Fulda, Hesse, Germany
m: 01 Feb 1798 in Hünfeld, Fulda, Hesse, Germany
d: 18 Nov 1822 in Hünfeld, Fulda, Hesse, Germany

Johann Joseph Drinnenberg

b: 25 Jan 1716 in Hunfeld, Hesse, Germany
m: 13 Oct 1744 in Hünfeld, Fulda, Hesse, Germany
d: 05 Jun 1793 in Hünfeld, Hesse, Germany

Andreas Drinnenberg

b: Abt. 1677
m: Abt. 1697 in Fulda, Hesse-Nassau, Germany
d: 05 Jun 1745 in Hünfeld, Fulda, Hesse, Germany

Elisabeth

b: Abt. 1679
d: 16 Apr 1724 in Hünfeld, Fulda, Hesse, Germany

Anna Sabina Klüber

b: Abt. 1724 in Eichenzell, Fulda, Hessen, Germany
d: 19 May 1796 in Hünfeld, Fulda, Hesse, Germany

Thomas Klüber

b: Abt. 1692
m:
d: 23 May 1733 in Eichenzell, Fulda, Hesse, Germany

Anna Barbara

b: Abt. 1697
d:

Johann Phillip Drinnenberg and Maria Barbara Köhler

John Phillip was born on June 27, 1766 at Hünfeld, the son of Joseph Drinnenberg and Sabina Klüber.

Translation: On the 27th of June, John Phillip, born of the legitimate marriage of Joseph Drinnenberg and Anna Sabina. Sponsored by H. V. Phillip Marshall.

Johann was a shoemaker by trade and would have maintained a shop in Hünfeld. He and Maria were married at Hünfeld on February 1, 1798.

Translation: At Hünfeld, on the first of this month, according to church doctrine, the marriage contract was announced at Trident Square. John Phillip Drinnenberg, legitimate son of Joseph Drinnenberg and Sabina, a legitimate daughter of the proper marriage of Klüber; and Maria Barbara Köhler, who is still living, the legitimate daughter of Paul Köhler and M. Margaretha ratified Abel by legitimate marriage. Witnessed by John Michael Aurtmann and Balthasar Huppel, citizens of Hünfeld.

Johann died at Hünfeld on November 18, 1822.

Translation: Entry 49, Hünfeld, Phillip Drinnenberg. On the 18th day of the month, Phillip Drinnenberg contracted a fever of the chest. He was a cobbler in Hünfeld and about 55 years old. He was buried with scared rites.

My 4ᵗʰ Great Grandparents
Johann Joseph Drinnenberg and Sabina Klüber

Johann Joseph was born on January 25, 1716 in Hünfeld.

Translation: On the 25th of this month is baptized John Jospeh, the son of Andreas Drinnenberg and Elisabeth, a maiden, of Hünfeld. Patron, John Joseph Manfell of Hünfeld.

He married Sabina Klüber of Hünfeld on October 13, 1744. Sabina's father was huntsman for the Prince-Abbott and it is likely that the family would have lived in a cottage on the grounds of the summer palace.

Translation: On the 13th, I united the honest young man Joseph, the legitimate son of Andreas Drinennberg, Senator, with the chaste virgin Anna Sabina, daughter of Thomas Klüber, Huntsman of the Prince Abbott in Eichenzell, a relict [meaning his wife was deceased]. Wittnesses were John Lanstein and Joseph George Krauss, citizens of Hünfeld.

John Joseph died at Hünfeld on June 5, 1793 at age 77. The detail captured by the Priest is rather amazing for the time period.

Translation: At Hünfeld on the 5th of this month, Joseph Drinnenberg was buried. He was a cobbler, an old man of 40 years. For a long time, he labored from the corruption of an infection and a difficulty of breathing. Finally, with fever, he went to a window for air, and according to his widow Sabina, suddenly stopped breathing.

Sabina died in Hünfeld on May 19, 1796 at age 72.

Translation: On the 19th of this month, Sabina was buried, a widow of 60 years of age. She was buried with scared rites.

My 5ᵗʰ Great Grandparents

Andreas Drinennberg and Elizabeth

Andreas Drinnenberg was born circa 1677. The records indicate that he married twice over the course of his lifetime.

His first wife, Elisabeth, was born circa 1680. Neither birth nor marriage records for her were identified. The christening records do indicate that Elisabeth is the mother of Johann Joseph, the 5ᵗʰ great grandfather of Walter Afield. She died on April 16, 1724 at Hünfeld.

Translation: On the 16th of this month in Hünfeld, Andreas Drinnenberg, by act of providence the Assessor of Eikenzell, 49 years of age.

His second wife was Anna Catharina Landstein. They were married on April 27, 1728.

Translation: The marriage contract was announced according to church law. On the 27th were married, Andreas Drinnenberg, a widow and a Sentor of Hünfeld, with a virtous virgin, Anna Catharine, a daughter of John Landstein, who was married according to church law. The marriage took place in Hünfeld in the sight of the whole church. Wittnesses John Blathasar, cobbler, and Martin Schrupp, citizens of Hünfeld.

Andreas as Senator and the Political Climate of the Time

The time in which Andreas served as a Senator and Lay Assessor would have been at the end of Frederick William I's reign (1713-1740) and into the beginning of Frederick II's reign (1740-1786). It was a volatile time on the European continent, with many rulers of independent territories trying to accumulate power; while at the same time, find harmony with the Holy Roman Empire.

The state of Brandenburg-Prussia became commonly known as "Prussia" during the reign of Frederick William I, who was known as the "Soldier King." He is considered the creator of the Prussian bureaucracy and created the standards for the professionalized army, which he developed into one of the most powerful in Europe. Also, Frederick William settled more than 20,000 Protestant refugees from Salzburg in thinly populated eastern Prussia.

The king died in 1740 and was succeeded by his son, Frederick II, whose accomplishments led to his reputation as "Frederick the Great". (H. W. Koch, A History of Prussia pp. 100–102.)

Frederick the Great practiced enlightened absolutism, referring to himself as "first servant of the state". He introduced a general civil code, abolished torture and established the principle that the Crown would not interfere in matters of justice. He also promoted an advanced secondary education, the forerunner of today's German gymnasium (grammar school) system, which prepares the brightest pupils for university studies. (Hans-Christof Kraus. Kultur, Bildung und Wissenschaft im 19. Jahrhundert. Oldenbourg Wissenschaftsverlag, 2008, p. 90) The Prussian education system was emulated in various countries, including the United States (Clark, Iron Kingdom, chapter 7).

In 1740, Prussian troops crossed over the undefended border of Silesia and occupied Schweidnitz. Silesia was the richest province of Habsburg Austria. This began the three Silesian Wars (1740–1763), which dominated German politics until 1866.

Andreas died at age 68 on June 5, 1745 at Hünfeld.

Translation: On the 5th day of this month, Andreas Drinnenberg, a widower, was buried with full ceremony and scared rites.

My 5ᵗʰ Great Grandparents

Thomas Klüber and Anna Barbara

The only record identified at the Fulda Archives is the death record of Thomas, who died at Eikenzell on May 23, 1733.

Translation: On the 23rd of May died Thomas Klüber, huntsman in Eikenzell, who was a pious member of the church and obeyed its teachings.

Life as Huntsman for the Prince-Abbott's

In his daughter's marriage record, we learn that Thomas is huntsman for the prince-abbot at the summer palace at Eikenzell, north of Fulda.

Throughout Western Europe, humans hunted wild animals. While game was at times an important source of food, it was rarely the principal source of food. Hunting was mostly a pastime of the aristocracy. It was an important arena for social interaction, essential training for war, and a privilege and measurement of nobility.

Most nobles kept, as a part of their estate, a large area of woodland "the royal forest" where populations of game animals were kept and watched over by gamekeepers. The common weapons used for hunting were the bow, crossbow, lance and spear. Bows were the most commonly used weapon until handheld firearms were introduced in the late 16th century. In addition to weapons, the sport of hunting depended on the assistance of certain domesticated animals, the horse, the hound and the hawk or falcon.

The huntsman would coordinate and organize all of these pieces for hunting parties or sometimes just be the guide for the prince-abbott.

Castle Fasanerie: The Summer Palace at Eikenzell

Around 1710, a modest castle was constructed at the direction of the Prince-Abbot, Adalbert von Schleifras. The official architect of the Abbey of Fulda was Johann Dietzenhofer, and the Baroque-styled castle is attributed to him.

Below is the front façade of the summer palace as it would have appeared to our ancestor, Thomas Klüber.

By 1730, an expansion of the castle was undertaken by Prince Abbot Adolph von Dalberg, who had a second courtyard built on the east side. In 1757, a dramatic expansion was undertaken by Prince Bishop Amand von Buseck, essentially enclosing the original castle within the castle complex.

The castle was used until the mid-19th century as a summer residence for the prince-bishop's. After the annexation by Prussia, the property was expropriated by the Prussian monarchy until 1878. Border changes reverted ownership to Friedrich Wilhelm who kept it as a private residence. His wife, Princess Anna of Prussia, occupied the complex until 1918.

During World War II, the castle suffered severe damage. After extensive restoration, portions of the castle were opened to the public in 1951. It now belongs to the Hessian House Foundation, which administers a large part of the art collection of the House of Hesse. These include a significant collection of antiques and an extensive porcelain collection.

The palace is a complex of several buildings and wings around a series of courtyards. The original building is flanked in the middle of the complex by two towers. The photo below shows the current configuration as the Drinnenberg's and Afeld's would have known it.

Attribution: By Efficiency at de.wikipedia (Transferred from de.wikipedia) [Public domain], from Wikimedia Commons.

My Great Great Grandmother
Anna Maria Drinnenberg
Her Mother's Line – Köhler and Marschall

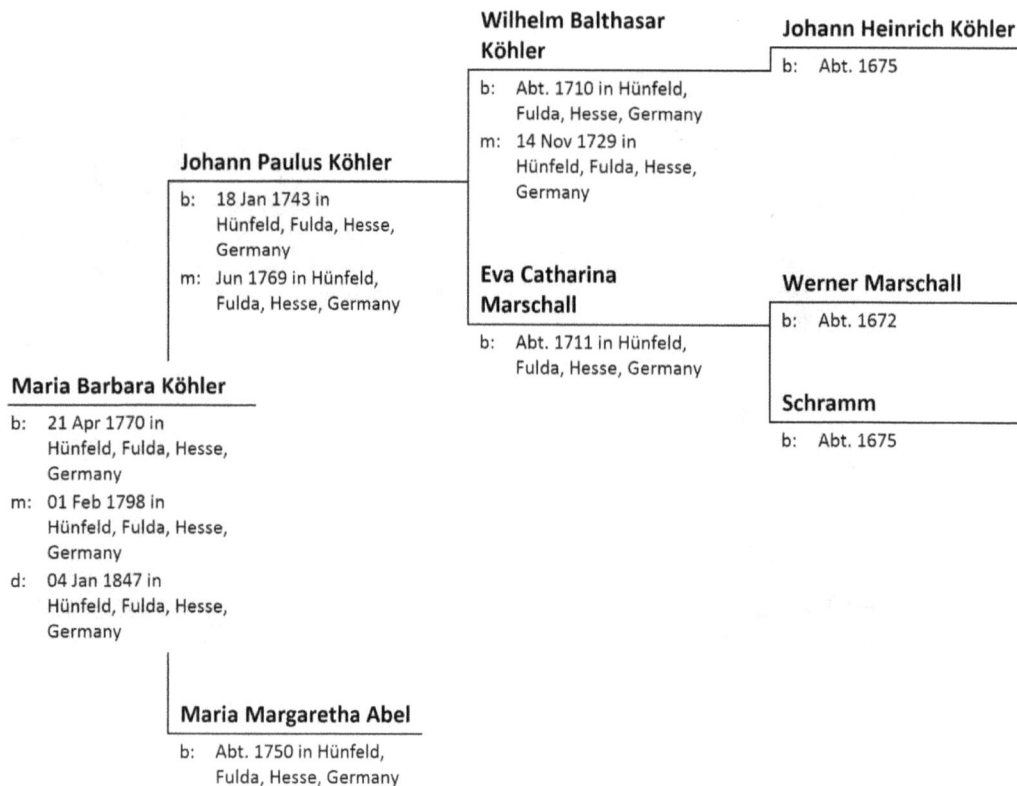

Wilhelm Balthasar Köhler
- b: Abt. 1710 in Hünfeld, Fulda, Hesse, Germany
- m: 14 Nov 1729 in Hünfeld, Fulda, Hesse, Germany

Johann Heinrich Köhler
- b: Abt. 1675

Johann Paulus Köhler
- b: 18 Jan 1743 in Hünfeld, Fulda, Hesse, Germany
- m: Jun 1769 in Hünfeld, Fulda, Hesse, Germany

Eva Catharina Marschall
- b: Abt. 1711 in Hünfeld, Fulda, Hesse, Germany

Werner Marschall
- b: Abt. 1672

Schramm
- b: Abt. 1675

Maria Barbara Köhler
- b: 21 Apr 1770 in Hünfeld, Fulda, Hesse, Germany
- m: 01 Feb 1798 in Hünfeld, Fulda, Hesse, Germany
- d: 04 Jan 1847 in Hünfeld, Fulda, Hesse, Germany

Maria Margaretha Abel
- b: Abt. 1750 in Hünfeld, Fulda, Hesse, Germany

My 3rd Great Grandmother
Maria Barbara Köhler

Maria Barbara was born on April 21, 1770 at Hünfeld to Johann Paulus Köhler and Maria Margaretha Abel.

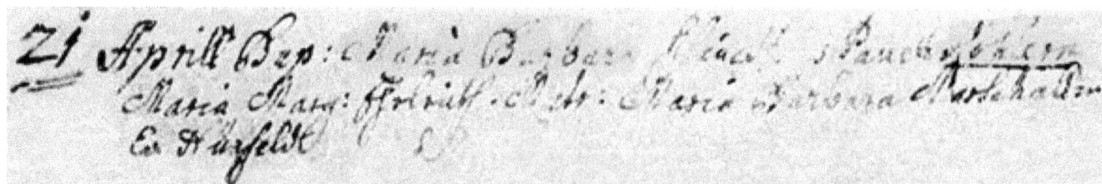

Translation: On the 21st of April was baptized Maria Barbara, the legitimate daughter of Paul Köhler and Maria Margaretha: Sponsor Maria Barbara Marshall of Hünfeld.

She died at age 76 on January 4, 1847 at Hünfeld.

Translation: Entry 931: Died January 4, age 67. Maria Barbara Drinnenberg was married to John Phillip Drinnenberg. She was born on April 21st, 1770 at Hünfeld. She is a widow of the shoemaker John Phillip.

My 4ᵗʰ Great Grandparents

Johann Paulus Köhler and Maria Margaretha Abel

Johann was born at Hünfeld on January 18, 1743.

Translation: On the 18th of this month, I married John Paul, the legitimate son of Wilhelm Balthasar Köhler and Eva Catharina who were legitimately married. He was sponsored by John Paul Marschall, a citizen of Wirtz.

They were married at Hünfeld in June 1769. The image for this record was too faint to print, but the translation is below.

Translation: In June I married John Paul Köhler with the virgin Maria Margaretha Ablel. Witnesses John Paul Köhler and John Joseph Drinnenberg of Hünfeld.

My 5th Great Grandfather and His First Wife

Marriage of Wilhelm Balthasar Köhler to Anna Maria Breüning

Translation: January [1728] - On the 27th of this month in front of the whole church at Hünfeld are honestly joined, Wilhelm Balthasar, adolescent son of Henry Köhler and his wife, who has left them behind [died], with Anna Maria, a modest virgin, daughter of the legitimate marriage of Valentin Breüning and his wife. Wittnesses, Balthasar Huppel and John Schramm, both of Hünfeld.

My 5th Great Grandparents

Wilhelm Balthasar Köhler and Eva Catharina Marschall

They were married on November 14, 1729 at Hünfeld. This is a second marriage for Wilhelm. Since it is performed in the church, his first wife must have died within the year following their marriage.

Translation: Hünfeld – On the 14th of this month are married Wilhelm Balthasar Köhler and Eva Catharina Marschall, an honest virgin, a legitimate child of Werner Marschall, a butcher. Witnesses: John Schramm and John Adam Hodes from Bingstann.

Chapter 12

The Ancestry of Olga C. Antony of Christiania, Norway

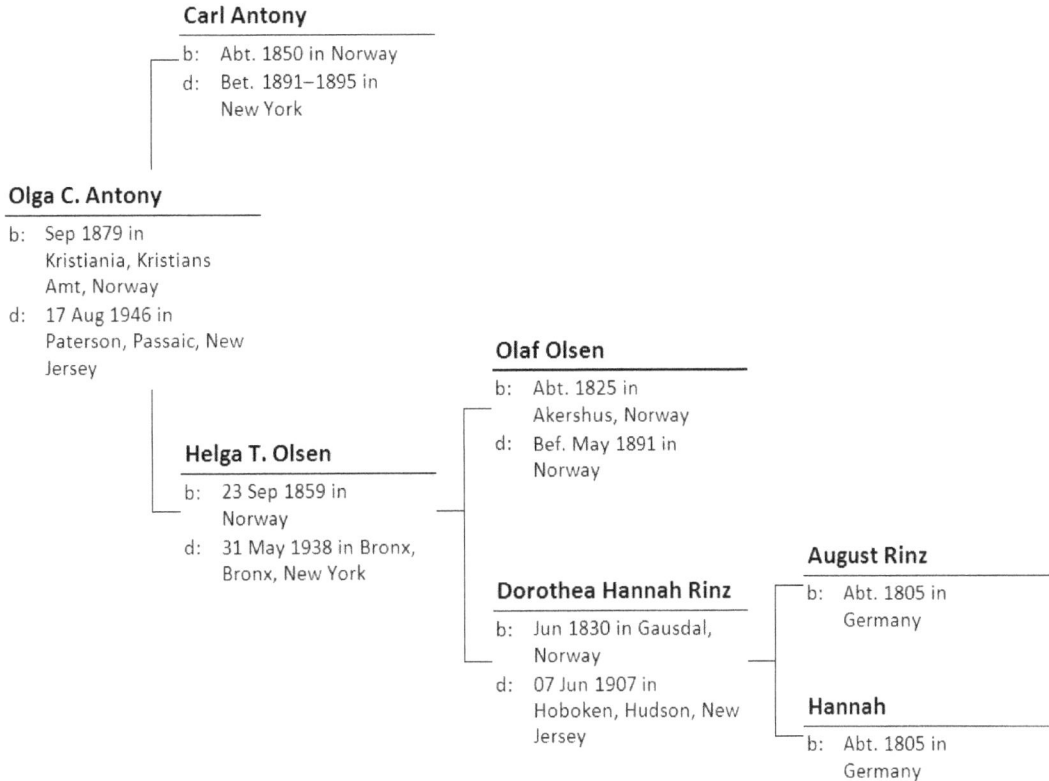

Carl Antony

- b: Abt. 1850 in Norway
- d: Bet. 1891–1895 in New York

Olga C. Antony

- b: Sep 1879 in Kristiania, Kristians Amt, Norway
- d: 17 Aug 1946 in Paterson, Passaic, New Jersey

Olaf Olsen

- b: Abt. 1825 in Akershus, Norway
- d: Bef. May 1891 in Norway

Helga T. Olsen

- b: 23 Sep 1859 in Norway
- d: 31 May 1938 in Bronx, Bronx, New York

Dorothea Hannah Rinz

- b: Jun 1830 in Gausdal, Norway
- d: 07 Jun 1907 in Hoboken, Hudson, New Jersey

August Rinz

- b: Abt. 1805 in Germany

Hannah

- b: Abt. 1805 in Germany

My Grandmother
Olga C. Antony

Olga C. Antony was born in Christiania, Norway, in what is present day Oslo. In the 1900 US Census, her mother gave her birth as September 1879.

This photo of Olga Antony Afeld was taken about 1939 in New Jersey.

Olga left her homeland on May 17, 1888, from the port of Christiania (Oslo). The ship traveled first to Copenhagen to pick-up additional passengers before crossing the Atlantic. She arrived in New York aboard the Hekla on June 1, 1888, with her mother. It is likely that her father, Carl, traveled ahead of them to get established, although it is difficult to distinguish him from many others with the same name on ship manifests and in the records overall. Antony and Olsen are very common surnames in Norway.

Courtesy of the Norway Heritage Collection - www.norwayheritage.com.

The Hekla was built by Scott's Shipbuilding & Engineering Company, Greenock, Scotland, in 1884 for Thingvalla Line. She weighed 3,258 gross tons and was 330 feet long by 41 feet wide. The maximum speed was 11 knots or 12.6 miles per hour. She accommodated 870 passengers (40 first class, 30 second class, 800 third class).

The Passenger Manifest showing Olga and Helga on lines 32 and 33.

Source Citation: Year: 1888; Arrival: New York, New York; Microfilm Serial: M237, 1820-1897; Microfilm Roll: Roll 520; Lines: 32 and 33; List Number: 732.

In June 1900, Olga is living at 1216 Park Avenue in Hoboken, New Jersey, at a boarding house with her mother. She was employed as a sales clerk in a China shop.

After the death of Norman, she married his brother, Eugene Louis Afeld. They are found living at 35 Maple Street in Passaic, New Jersey in 1910. Three children are included in the household, Walter, Robert, and Helen. Eugene and Olga indicate that this is a first marriage for both of them, so it may be that Olga and Norman did not have the opportunity to wed before his death. Eugene is a clerk in a Drygoods store.

The 1940 US Census indicates that the highest school grade she completed was 6th, so her formal education would have been before immigration. It also indicates that she was a naturalized citizen, although no record has been found.

Olga died on August 17, 1946 while visiting family in New Jersey.

Mrs. Eugene L. Afeld

Mrs. Olga C. Antony Afeld, 88, formerly of 209 Howe Avenue, Passaic, and wife of Eugene L. Afeld, of Gulfport, Fla., died Saturday in Patterson General Hospital after a week's illness. Mr. and Mrs. Afeld were visiting in the North for the summer when she was taken ill. Last September they gave up their Passaic residence, which they had occupied for 45 years, and moved to Florida.

Mrs. Afeld, who was born in Oslo, Norway, came to this country as girl. Mr. Afeld who is retired, was formerly with the New York office of the Barbour Linen Thread Company, Patterson. Surviving, in addition to Mr. Afeld, are three children, Mrs. Winthrop C. Wood, of Bloomfield; Walter and Robert Afeld, of Clifton, and five grandchildren. A funeral service will be held tomorrow.

(Source: Herald News, Monday, August 19, 1946, page 4. Now the New Jersey Herald)

STATE OF NEW JERSEY
VITAL RECORDS ABSTRACT CERTIFICATION

This document **IS NOT** a true certified copy and is issued for informational purposes only.

PLACE OF DEATH NEW JERSEY DEPARTMENT OF HEALTH—BUREAU OF VITAL STATISTICS	Registrar's No. *1099*

PLACE OF DEATH

County: Passaic

Township:

City or Borough: Paterson

Name of Hospital or Institution: Paterson General Hospital
(If not in hospital or institution write street number or location)

Length of Stay in this Community: 2 yrs. mos. days hrs.

Kindly Type or Print
FULL NAME MRS. Olga Afeld
(Surname last, first name here)

FORMER OR USUAL RESIDENCE

State: Florida   County:

City or Borough: Gulfport
(If outside city or borough limits, name township)

Street No. 5018-31 Ave. South
(If rural give location)

Citizen of If so, name foreign country? country

IF VETERAN, NAME WAR

SEX	COLOR OR RACE	Single, Married, Widowed or Divorced (write the word)
Female	White	Married

If married, widowed or divorced
HUSBAND OF
(Give full maiden name)
(or) WIFE OF: Eugene L Afeld   Age, if living: 73

BIRTH DATE OF DECEASED
(Month, day and year): January 13 1878

AGE Years	Months	Days	If less Than One Day	Hrs. Min.
68				

BIRTHPLACE (City or town): Oslo
(State or country): Norway

USUAL OCCUPATION: Housewife

Industry or business:

FATHER
NAME: Carl Antony
BIRTHPLACE (City or town): Oslo
(State or country):

MOTHER
MAIDEN NAME: Helga Olsen
BIRTHPLACE (City or town): Oslo
(State or country): Norway

SIGNATURE OF INFORMANT: Eugene L Afeld
(Address): 5018-31 Ave. South, Gulfport, Florida

PLACE OF BURIAL Cremation or Removal: St. Michaels Churchyard Cem
DATE: August 21 1946   Woodside, New York

FUNERAL DIRECTOR: Charles M. Morris   N.J. License No. 190
(Address): 106 Broadway, Passaic, N.J.

RECEIVED AUG 19 1946   Local Registrar.

MEDICAL CERTIFICATION

DATE OF DEATH: 8/17   1946

I HEREBY CERTIFY, That I attended the deceased from 8/9 1946 to 8/17 1946 that I last saw her alive on 8/17 1946 and that death occurred on the date stated above, at 9:38 P.M.

Due to:

Other conditions
(Include pregnancy within 3 months of death)

Major findings: Of operations

Of autopsy

PHYSICIAN
Underline the cause to which death should be charged statistically.

If death were due to external causes, fill in the following:

Accident, suicide, or homicide (specify):

Date of occurrence:

Where did injury occur:
(City or town) (County) (State)

Did injury occur in or about home, on farm, in industrial place, in public place?
(Specify type of place)

While at work? Means of injury:

Signature: John L. Framor, M.D.
(M.D. or other)

Address: Paterson Gen. Hospital   8/17/46
Date signed

Source: Department of Health and Senior Services, Bureau of Vital Statistics and Registration, Trenton, NJ.

135

Carl Antony and Helga T. Olsen

Carl Antony			Helga T. Olsen		
Born:	Abt. 1850		Born:	23 Sep 1859	
	Norway			Norway	
Died:	Bet. 1891–1895		Died:	31 May 1938	
	New York			Bronx, Bronx, New York	

Marriage:

Children:	Sex	Birth	Death
Olga C. Antony	F	Sep 1879 Kristiania, Kristians Amt, Norway	17 Aug 1946 Paterson, Passaic, New Jersey
Henry Antony	M	16 Jun 1890 Hoboken, Hudson, New Jersey	
Unknown Antony	?		Bef. Jun 1890

A son, Henry, was born to Carl and Helga on June 16, 1890.

Source: New Jersey State Archives. Record Group: Department of Health, Bureau of Vital Statistics. Series: Birth Certificates and Indexes, 1878-1923. Volume: 32 c.f. [64 vols. and 1 folder]; 1020 reels.

The birth certificate was completed by the Midwife who delivered Henry. It is interesting in that it is roughly half in German and half in English. We also learn that Carl's occupation is "engineer" and that Helga has given birth to three children and two are now alive, a fact that is later confirmed in the 1900 US Census.

Sometime between the birth of Henry in 1890 and 1895 (the year a New Jersey City Directory records Helga as "widow"), Carl dies, leaving Helga with Olga and her brother Henry to care for. This may explain why her mother, Hannah Olsen, emigrates in 1891 and appears in the household with them in 1900.

Household of Helga Antony in 1900 US Census

Surname	Given Name	Relationship	Age	Marital Status	Birthplace	Father's Birthplace	Mother's Birthplace	Immigration Year
Antony	Helga	Head	40	Widowed	Norway	Norway	Norway	1888
Olsen	Hannah	Mother	69	Married	Norway	Norway	Norway	1891
Antony	Olga	Daughter	20	Single	Norway	Norway	Norway	1888
Antony	Henry	Son	9	Single	New Jersey	Norway	Norway	

Source Citation: Year: 1900; Census Place: Hoboken Ward 5, Hudson, New Jersey; Roll: 974; Page: 14A; Enumeration District: 0048; FHL microfilm: 1240974.

By 1915, Helga marries Herman Behn, an immigrant who was born in Prussia. They are recorded in the New York State Census residing at 2668 Briggs Avenue, New York. This is a second marriage for both. It appears that Herman dies before the enumeration of the 1925 New York State Census, as Helga is recorded as head of household at 153 Logan Street in Brooklyn.

She is recorded at the same address in the 1930 US Census and indicates that she is renting the apartment for $40 per month and that she does not own a radio, a unique census question that was only asked in 1930.

Helga with her great grandson, Hollis Afield, in 1935.

Helga dies on May 31, 1938 from heart disease at age 79.

She is buried at Flower Hill Cemetery in Block Q, Row 17, Grave 20. The cemetery address is 5433 Kennedy Boulevard, North Bergen, New Jersey. She and her mother are interred together in the same plot.

Olaf Olsen and Dorothea Hannah Rinz

Hannah emigrated in 1891 from Norway, arriving at New York on May 29th. She traveled on the same ship (SS Hekla) that her daughter and granddaughter did in 1888. She died on June 7, 1907 and was buried at Flower Hill Cemetery in North Bergen, New Jersey on June 10th. Her grave is in Block Q, Row 17, Grave 20. She is buried with her daughter, Helga.

Source: New Jersey State Archives. Record Group: Department of Health, Bureau of Vital Statistics. Series: Death Certificates and Indexes, May 1848 to December 1913.